SCAN THIS BOOK TWO

Compiled by John Mendenhall

ART DIRECTION BOOK COMPANY

ISBN: 0-88108-193-0
LCCN: 91-077465

Printed in the United States of America

Published by:
Art Direction Book Company
456 Glenbrook Road
Glenbrook, CT 06906

Legal issues regarding copyright infringement are of increasing concern to the graphic design and advertising professional. The widespread availability of scanners has made the unauthorized reproduction of images a common occurrence. This has led to a growing number of lawsuits by owners of copyrighted material who prosecute those who steal their work. Court verdicts generally always favor the original creator, or their estate.

To avoid problems, one should be certain that the images being copied are not under copyright protection. While many believe that altering a copyrighted image in a photo manipulation program such as Adobe Photoshop is a way of circumventing the copyright law, this is not the case. Actually, in so doing one faces additional damages of destroying the integrity and value of the original work.

The images in this collection have been selected because they have fallen into public domain or were never under copyright to begin with. Purchasers of this book, and the first volume, have thousands of unique objects to choose from. Rather than just one or two clocks, for example, dozens are reproduced. Many clip art CD ROM collections give you just one of each object, making the chance that someone else uses it highly probable. This can be a problem in important jobs where originality is expected. When there are multiple variations to select from, the possibility of repetition diminishes.

Another excellent use of this book is as a reference for illustrating your own designs. Scan an image into a program such as Adobe Illustrator, and by using the template option you can draw your own version of it in digital form. Delete the original and you have a unique creation which in turn can be copyrighted.

The objects in the <u>Scan This Book</u> series have been selected for their usefulness. Being old, they avoid the tackiness inherent in many modern clip art collections. Time is precious for active designers. When you need an obscure image now, this collection will be there for almost any graphic design need.

Enjoy guilt-free scanning!

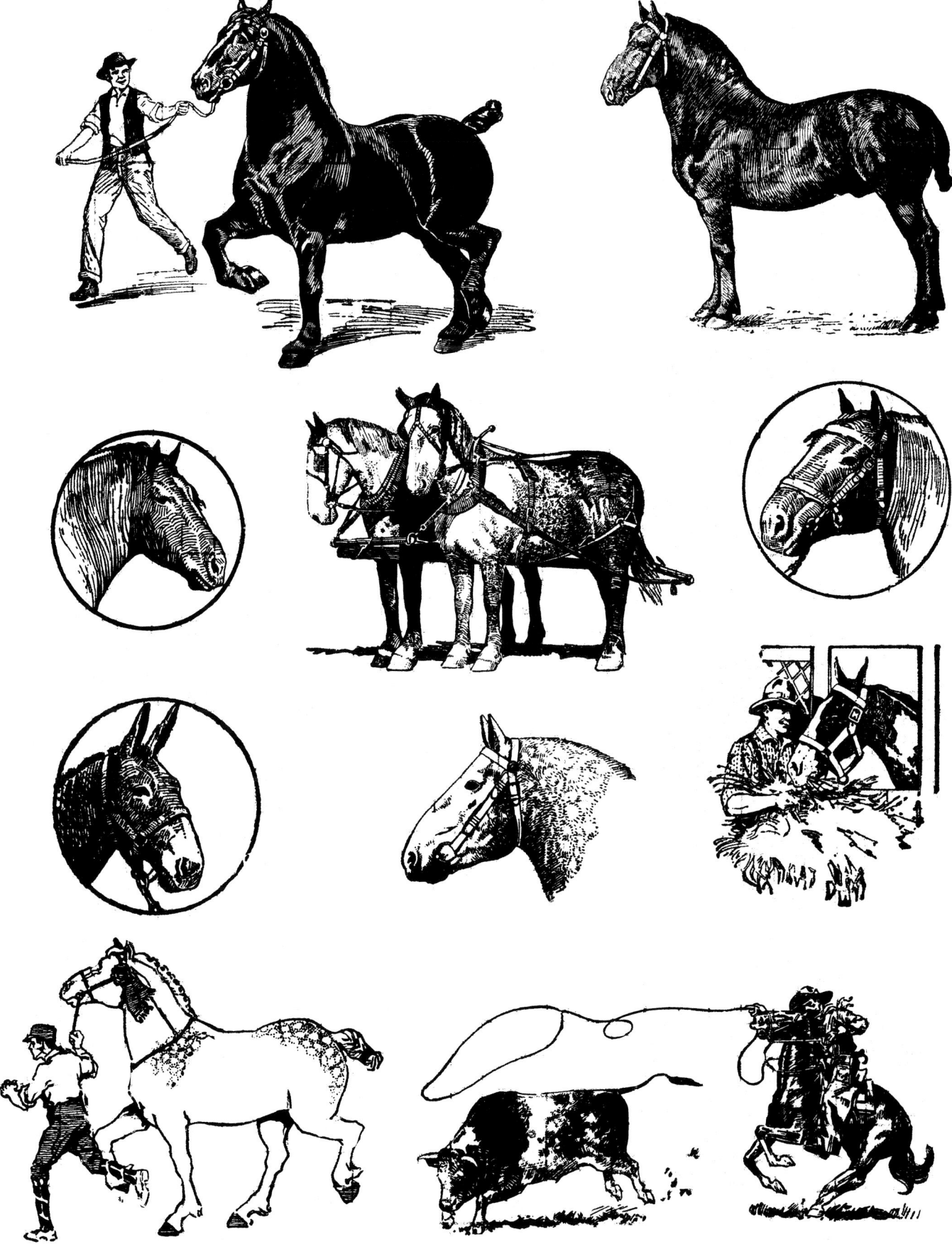

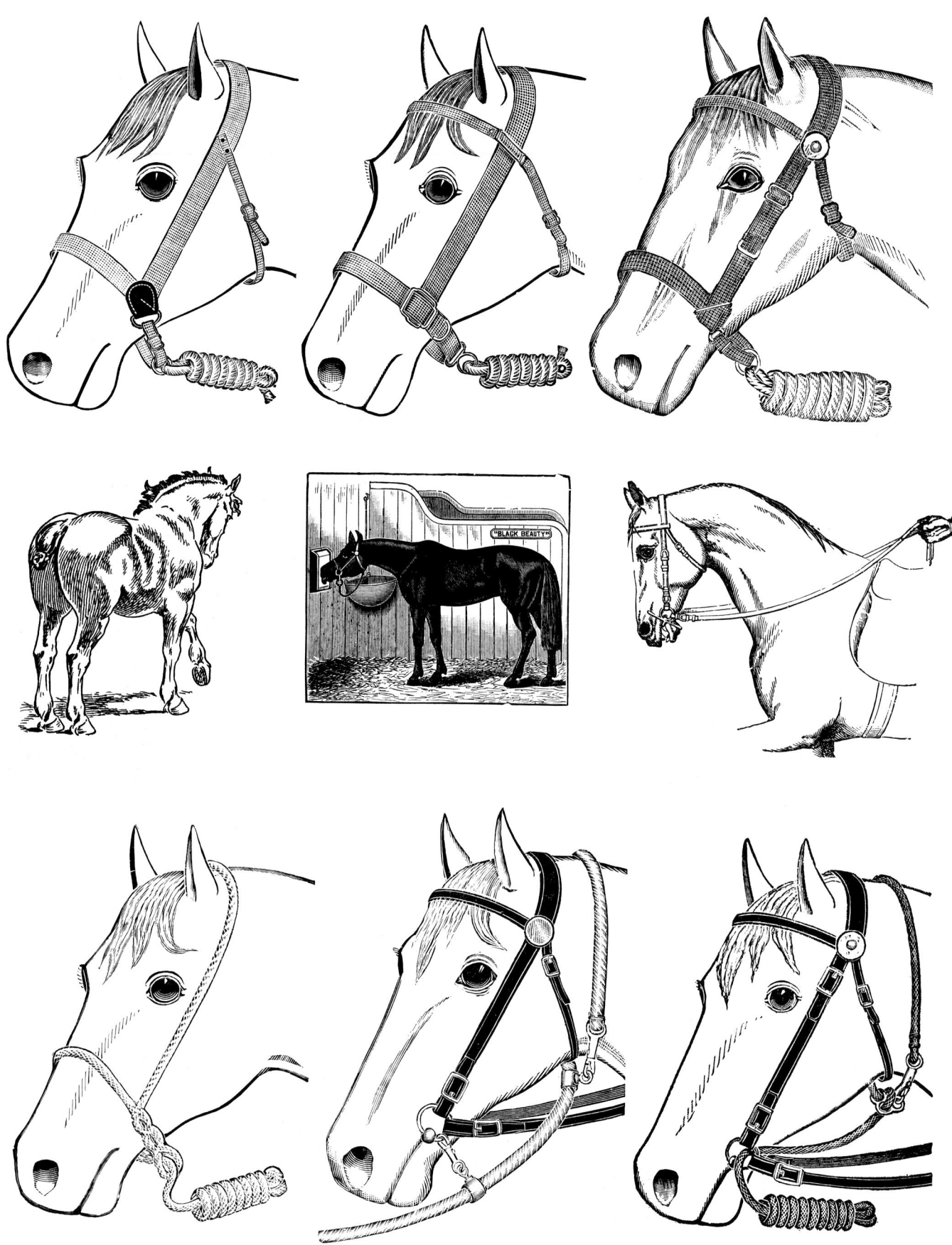

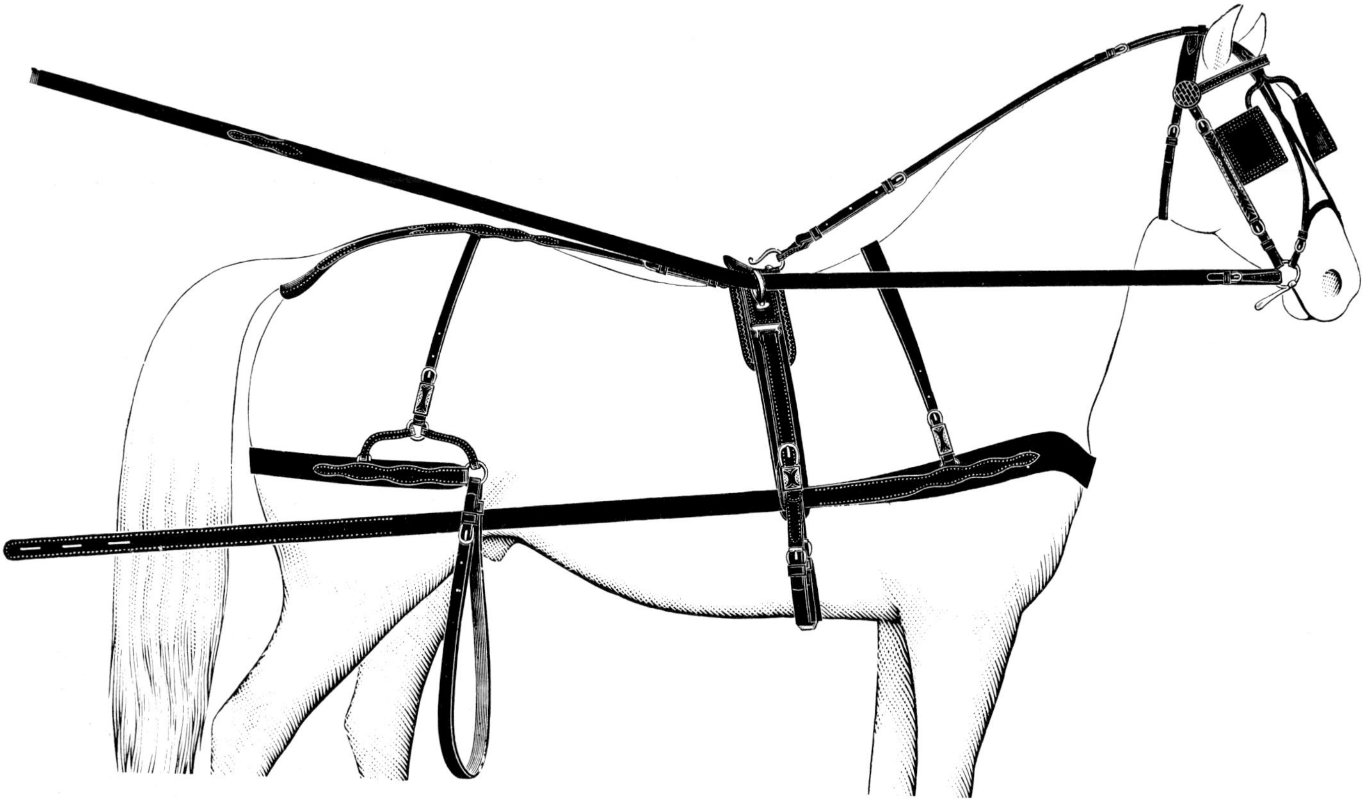

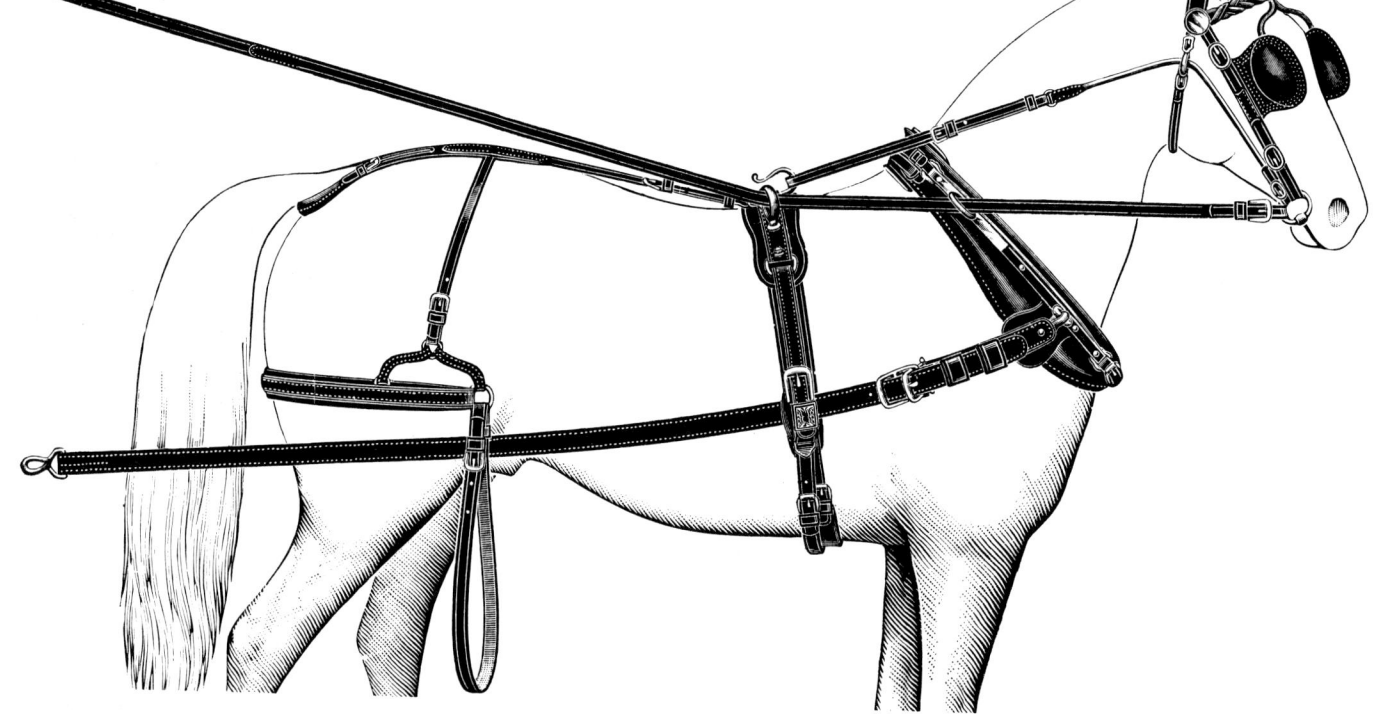

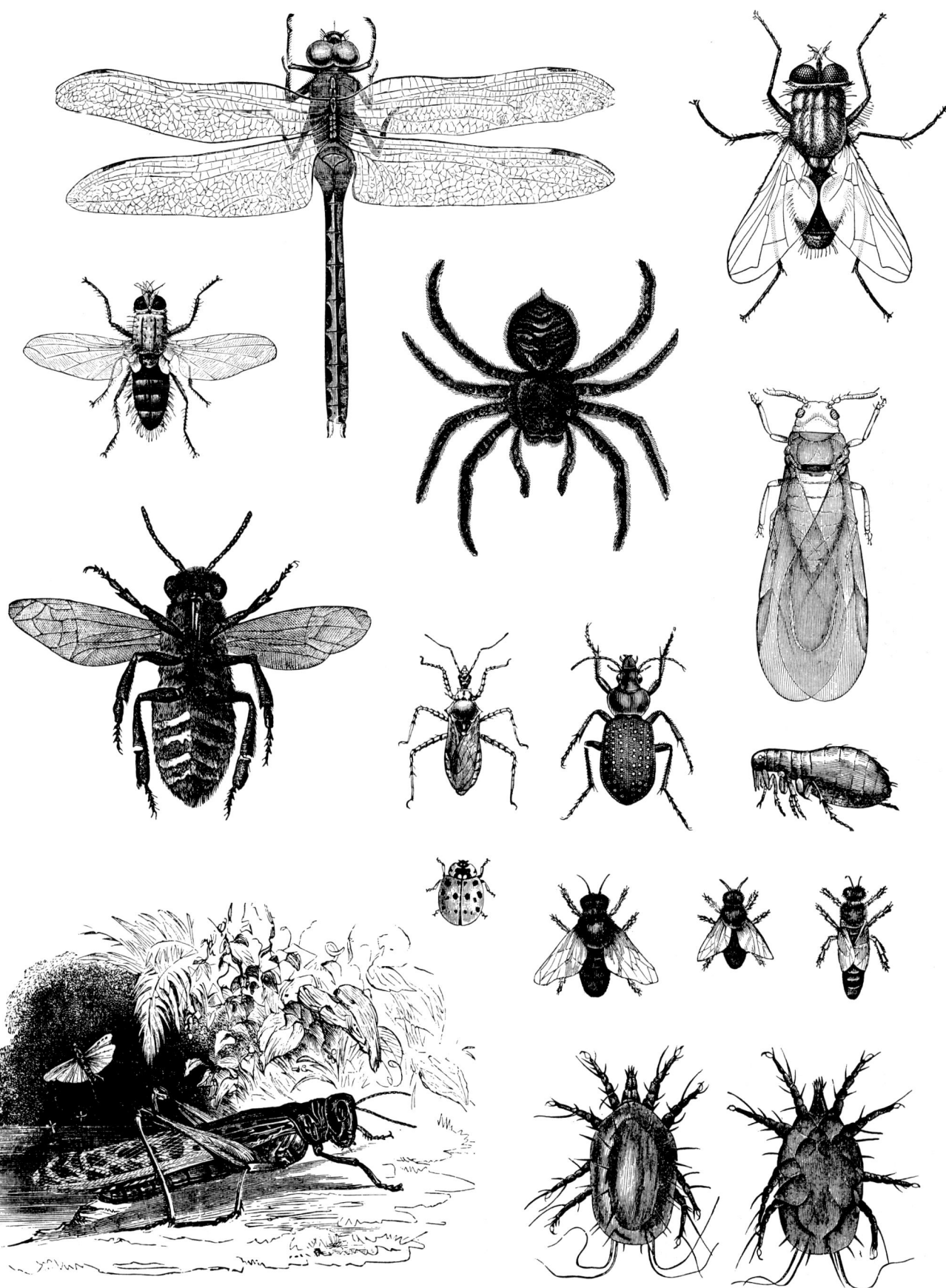

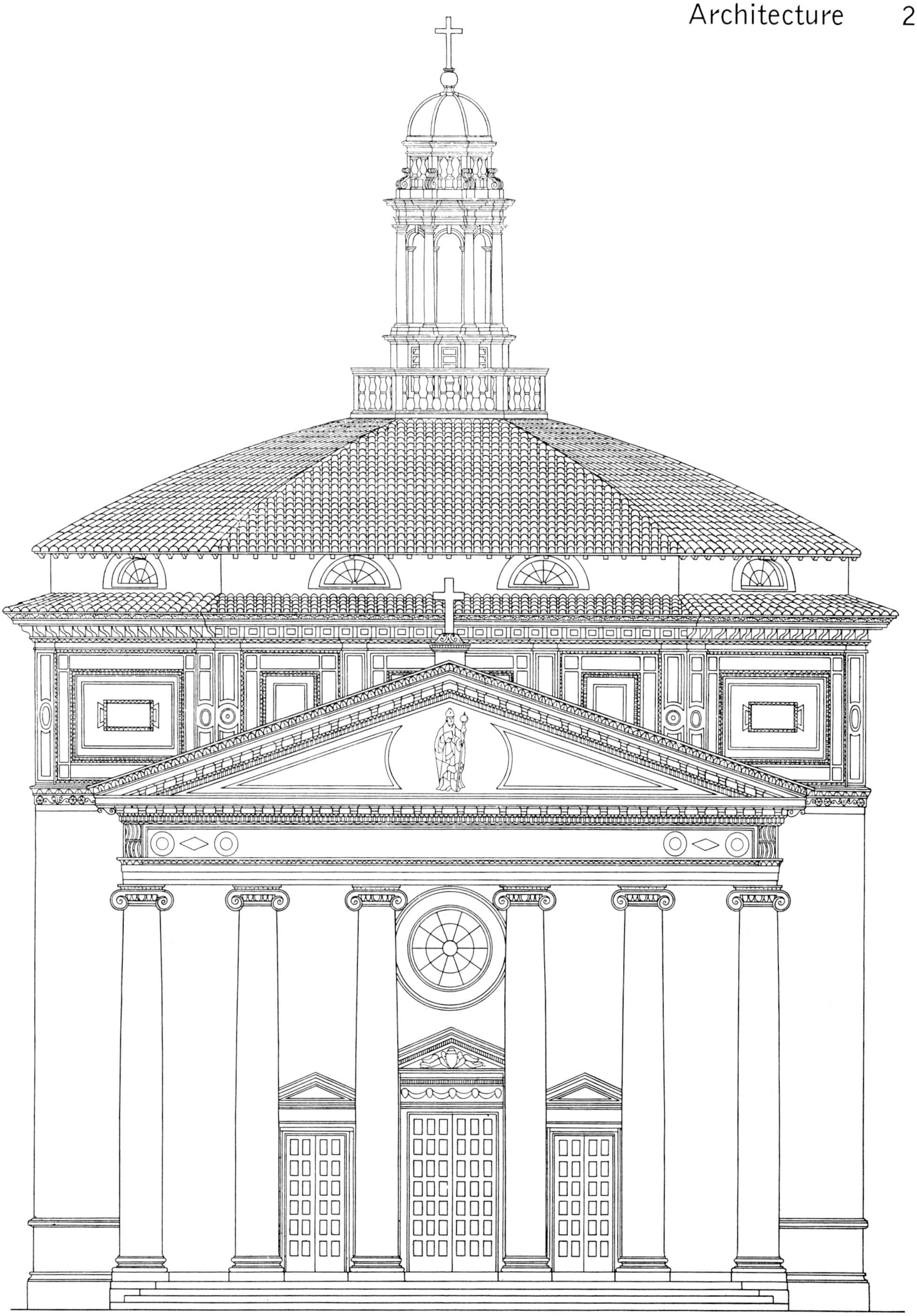

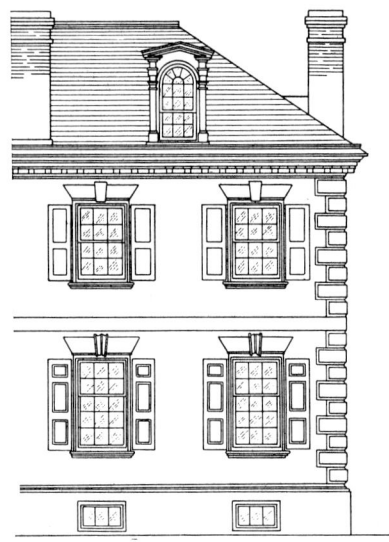

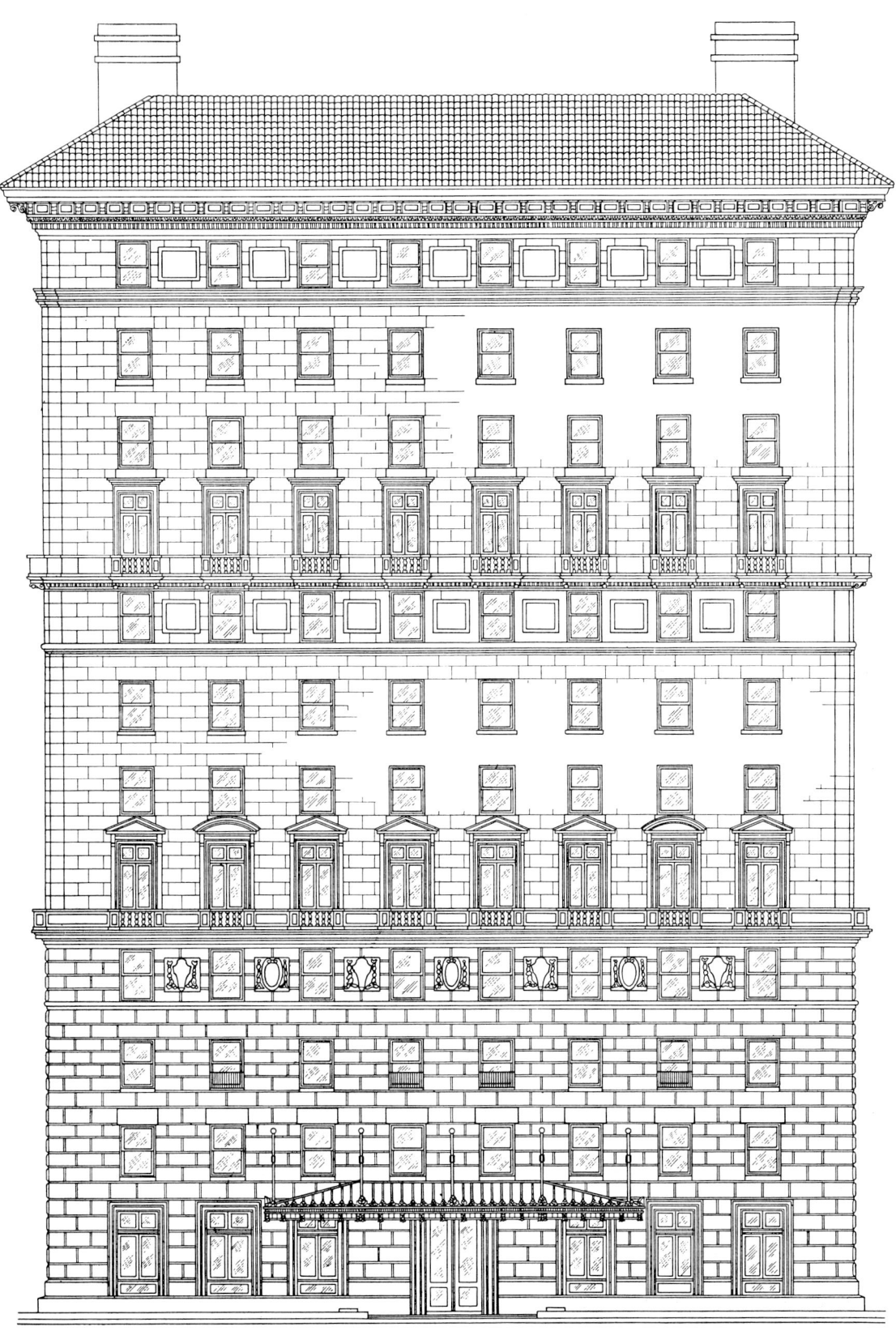

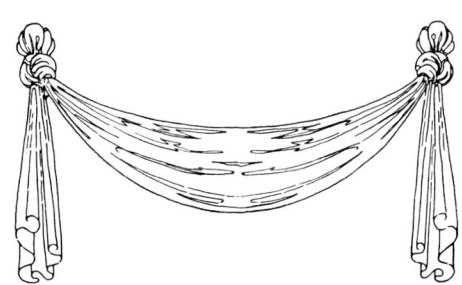

STATIONERS & PRINTERS

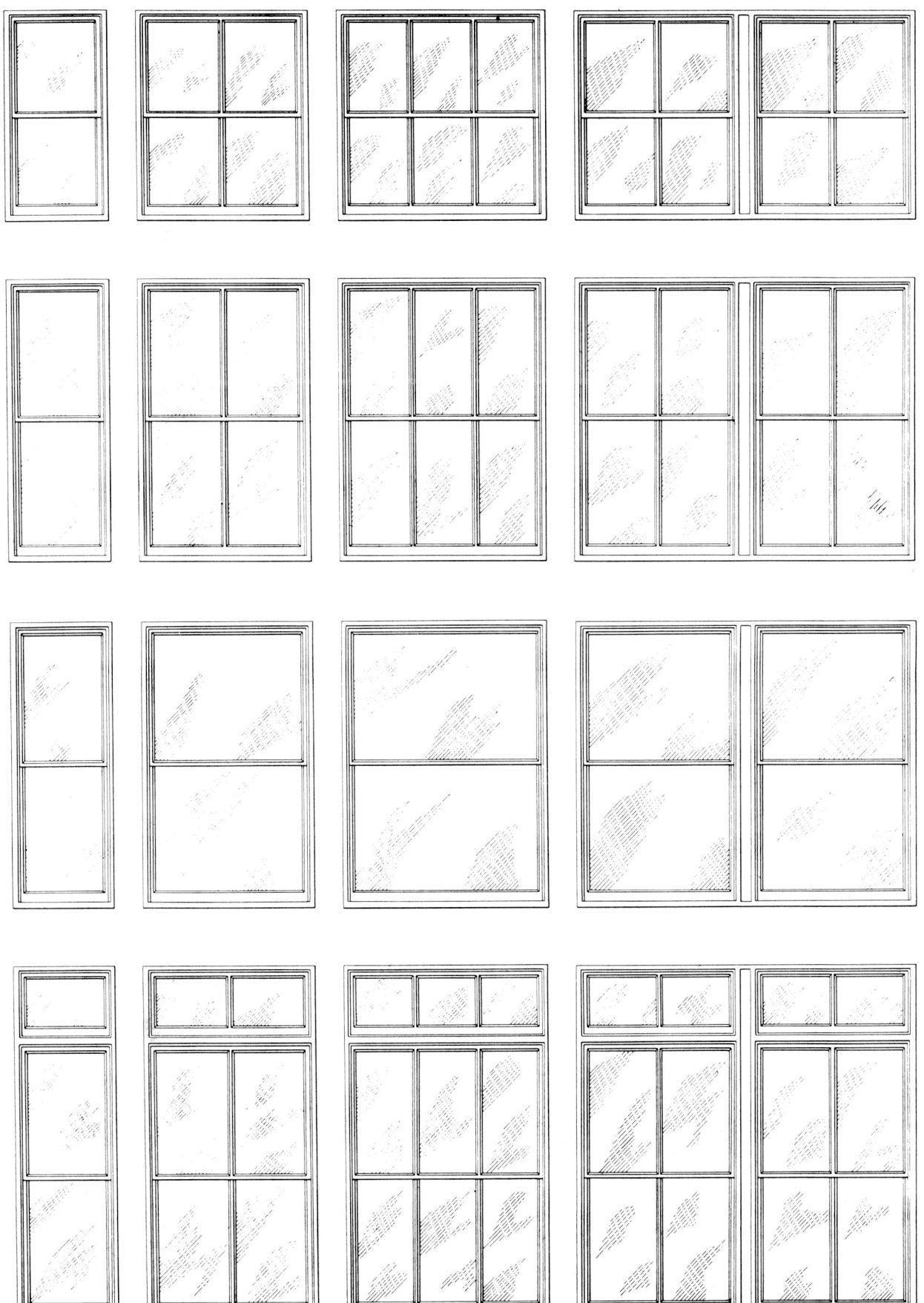

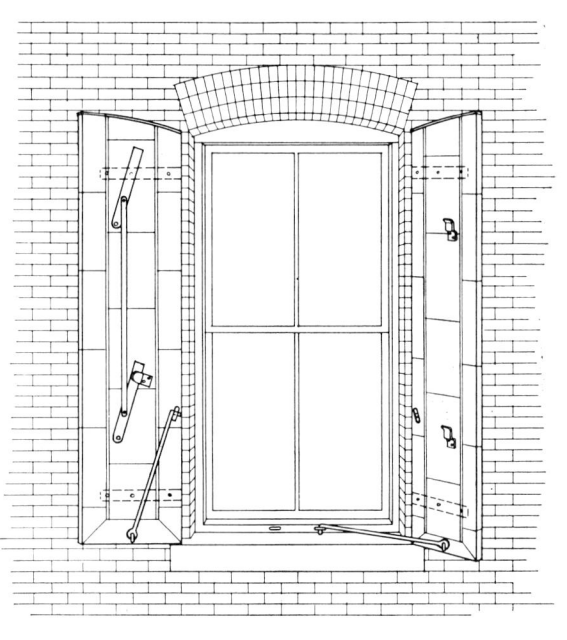
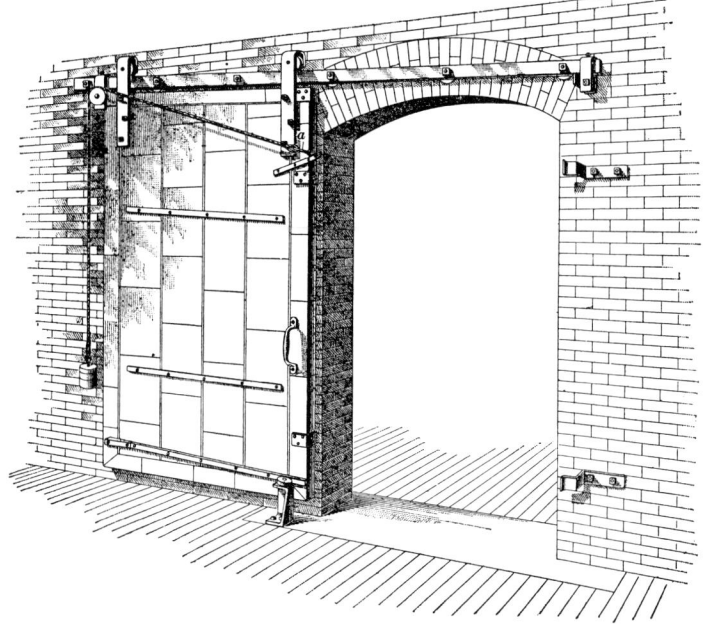
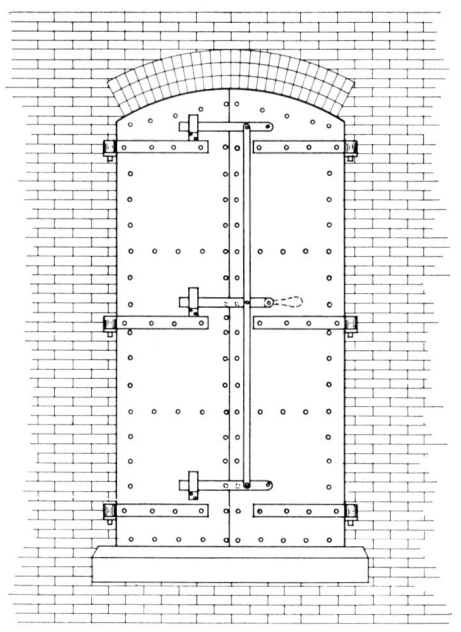

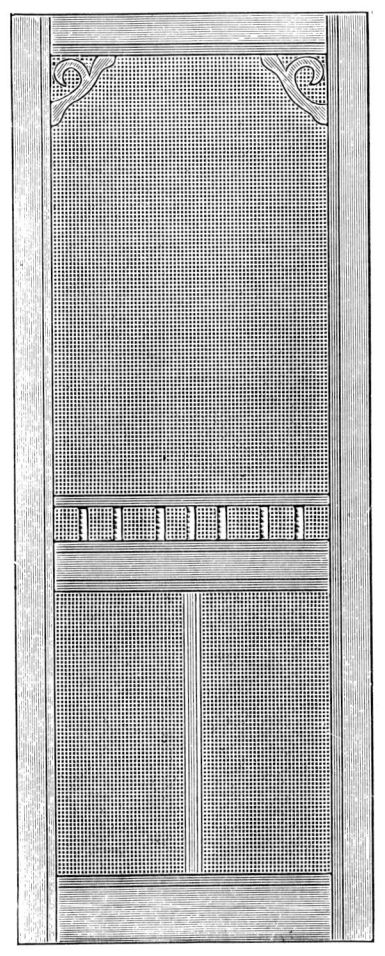

Corinthian   Tuscan   Doric   Ionic

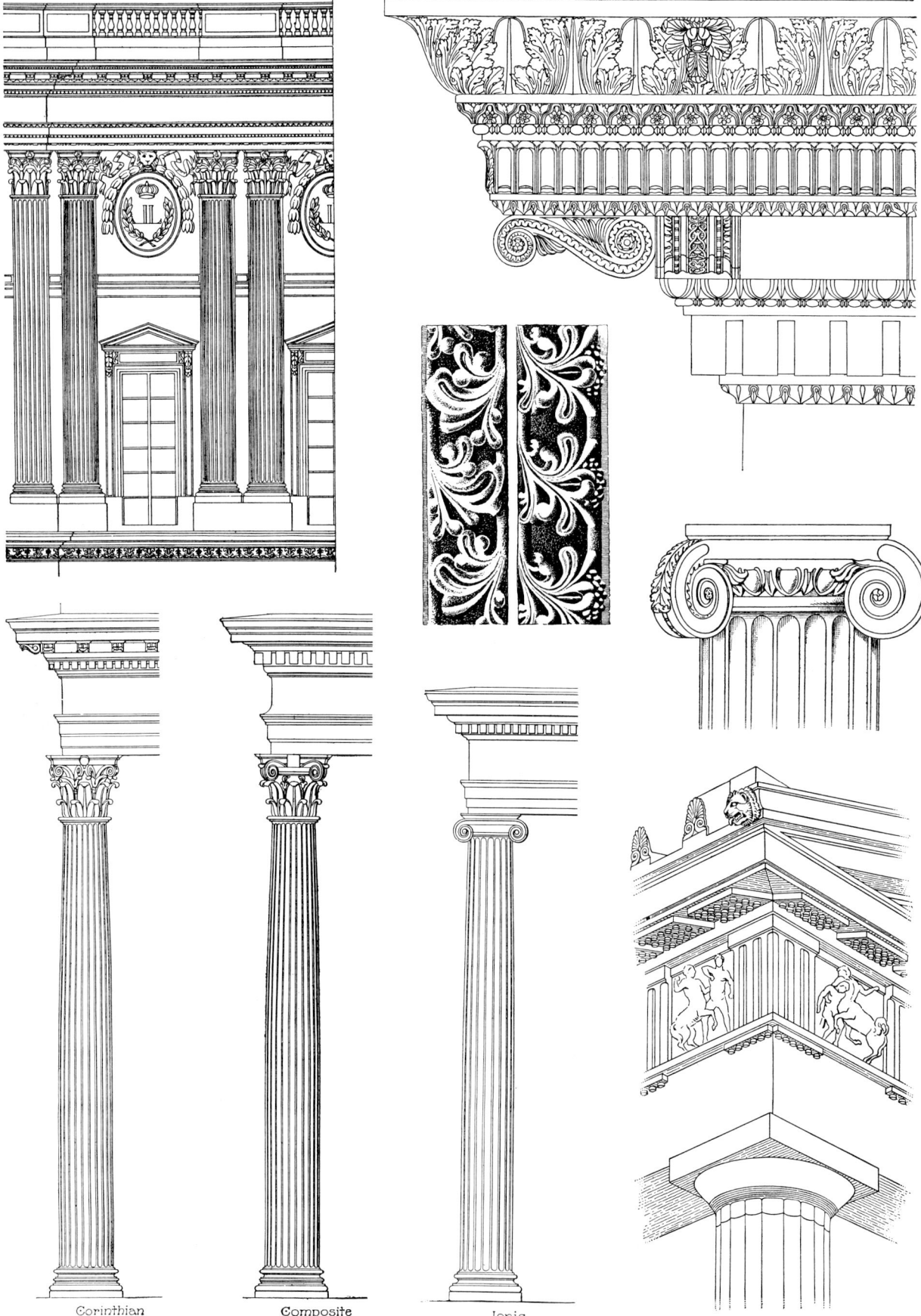

Corinthian   Composite   Ionic

SENAT CONS ANDRE
AE DE ORIA PATRIAE
LIBERATORI MVNVS
PVBLICVM

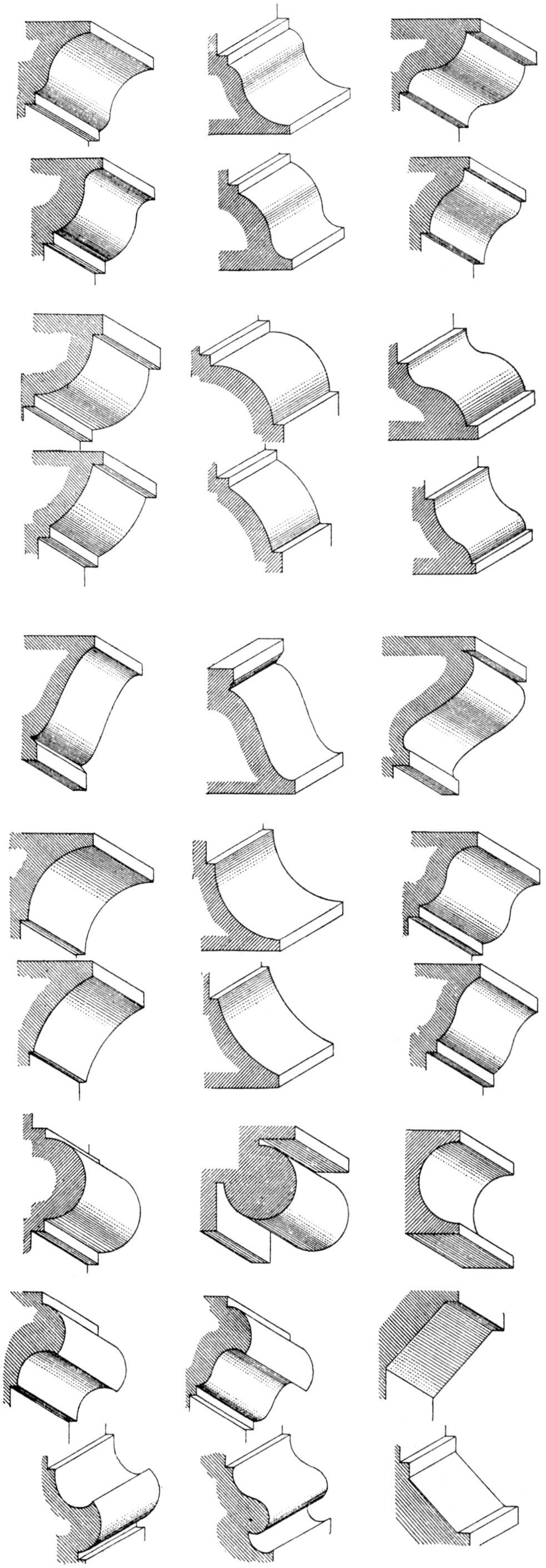

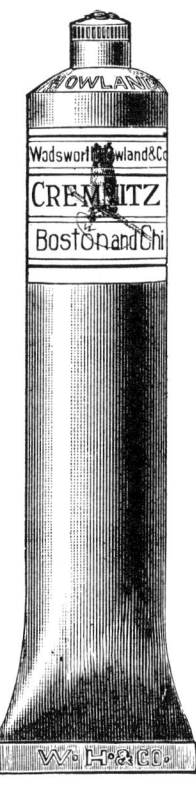

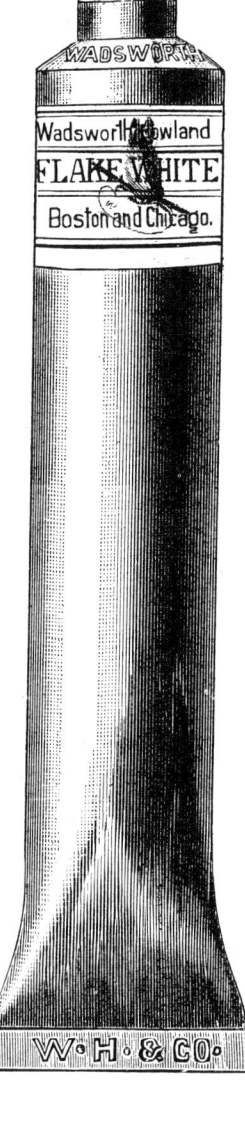

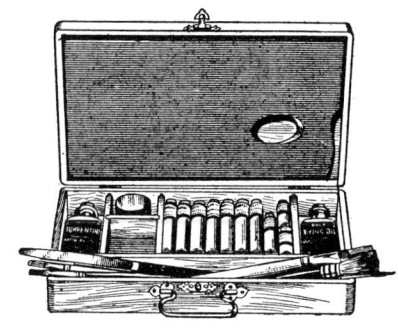

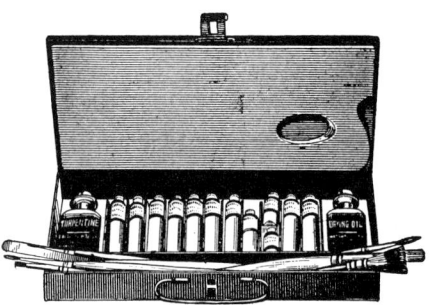

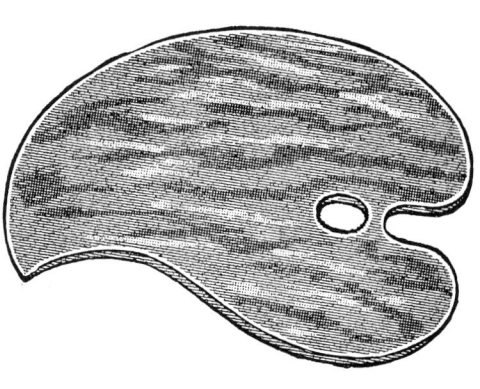

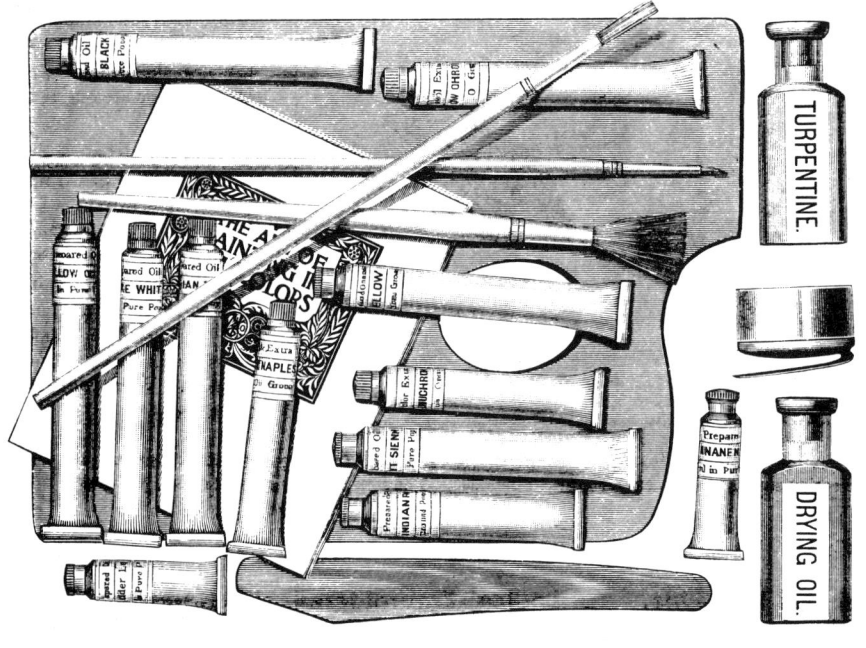

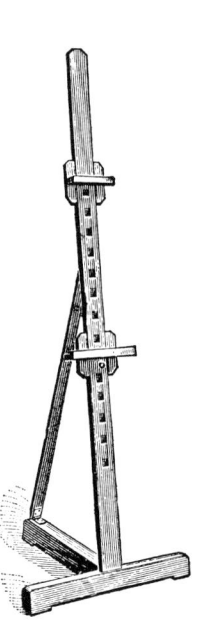

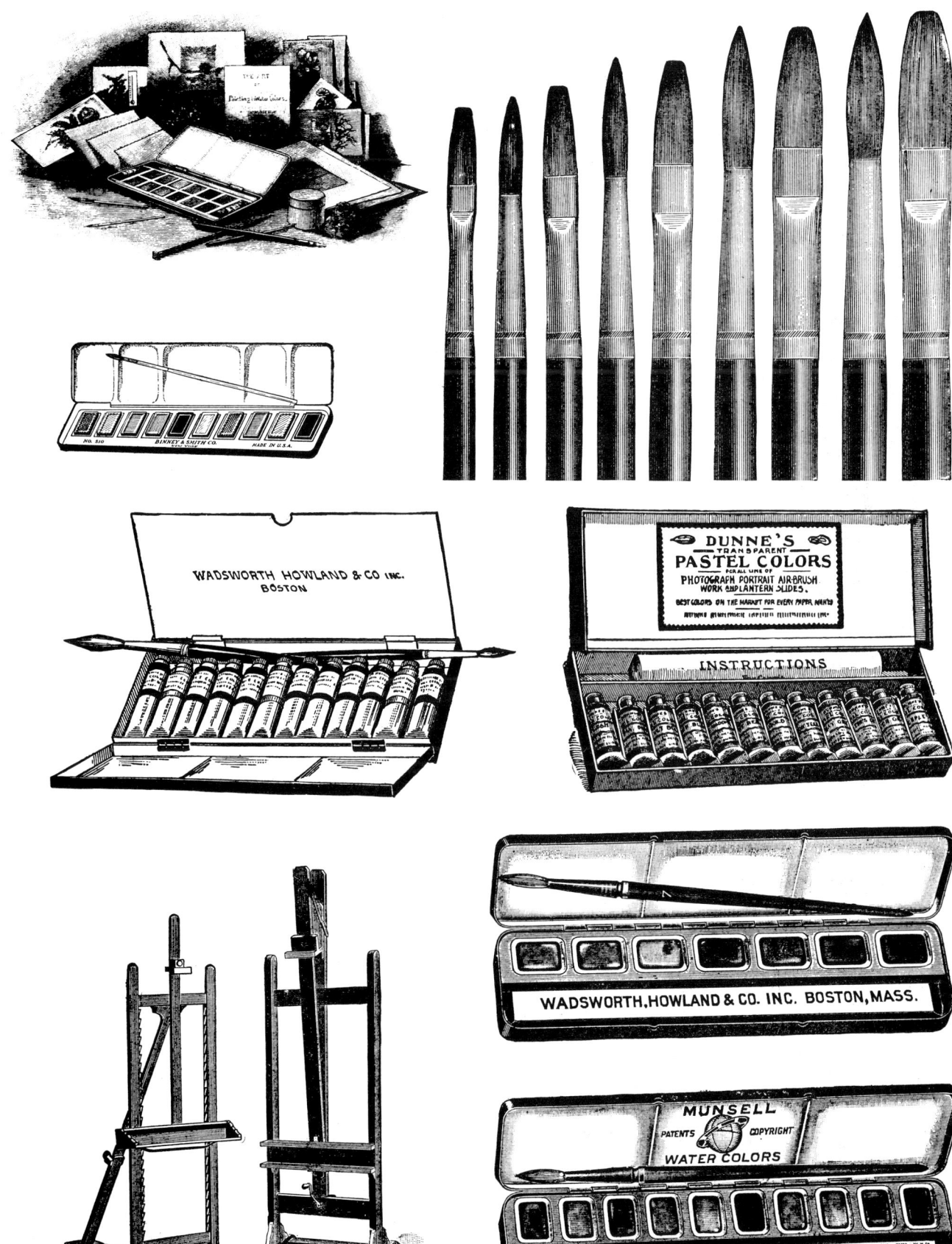

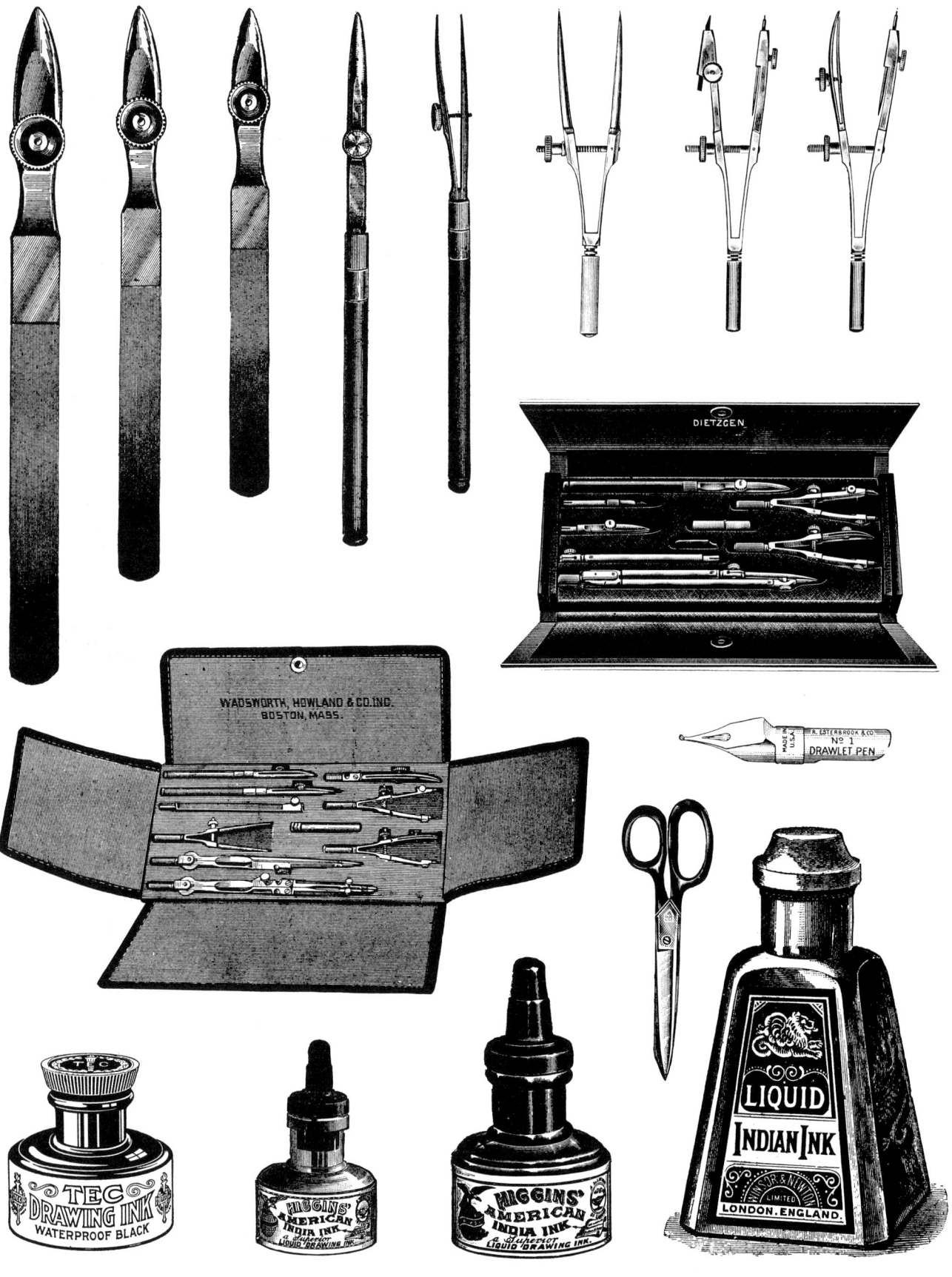

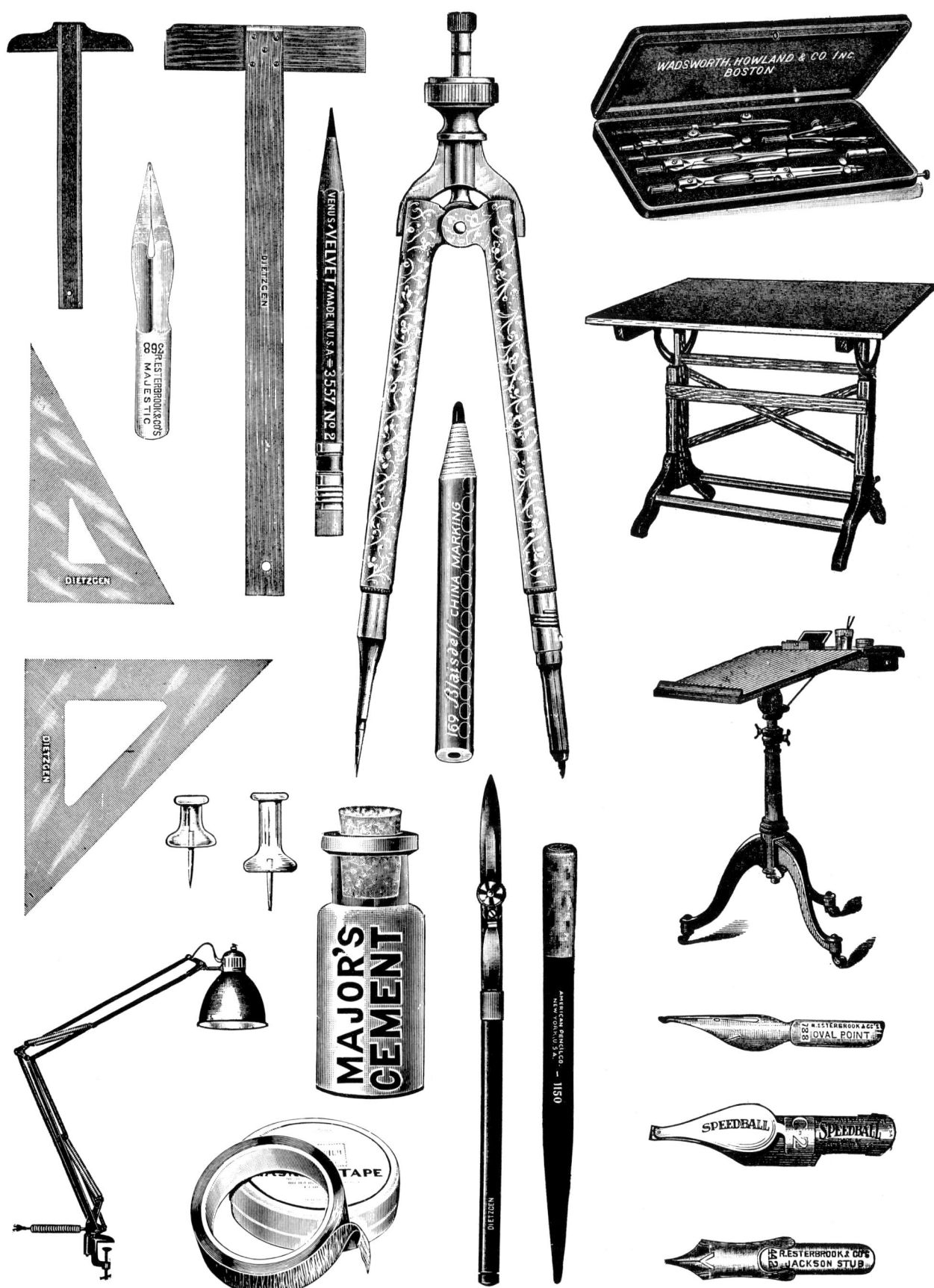

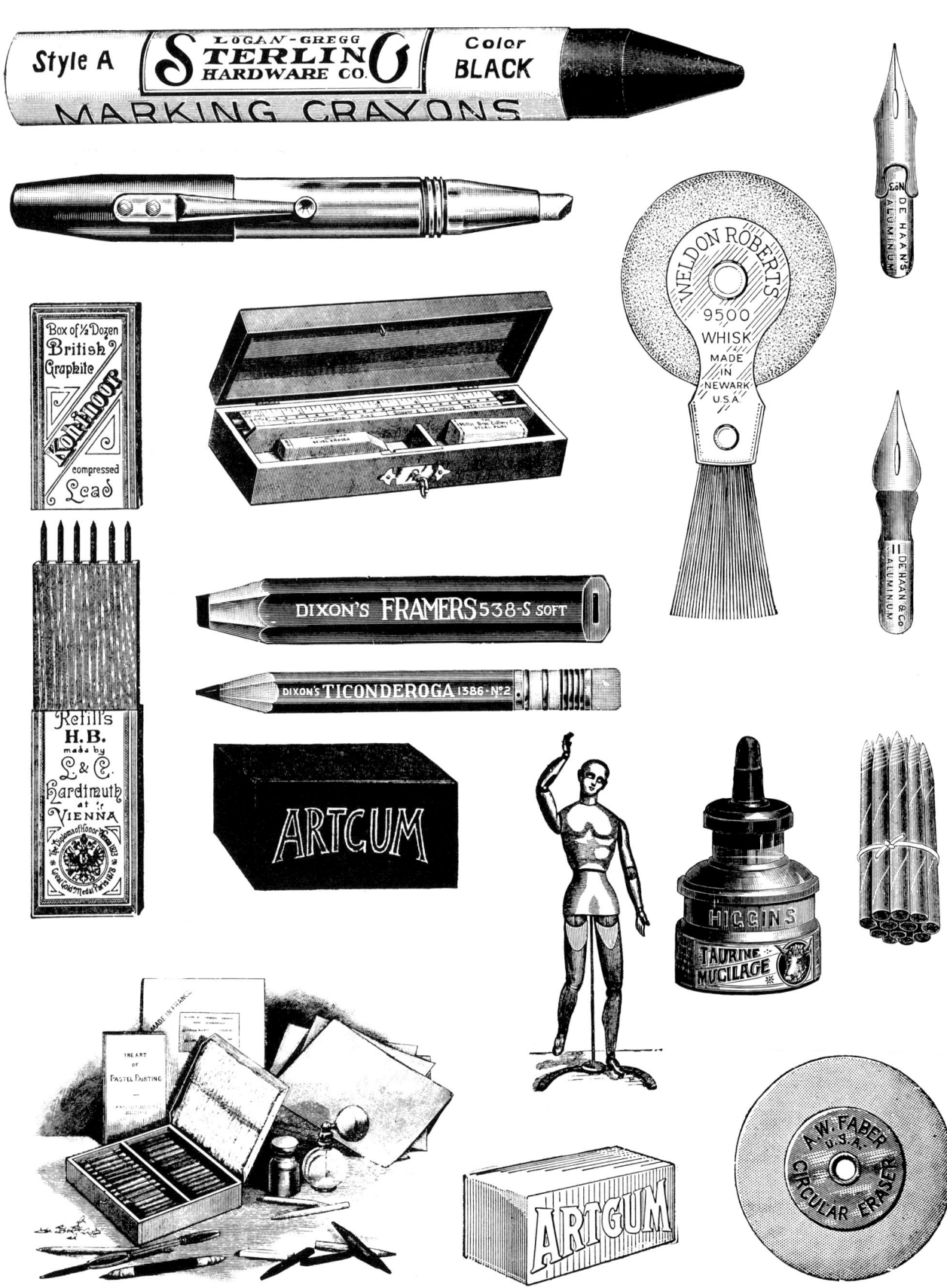

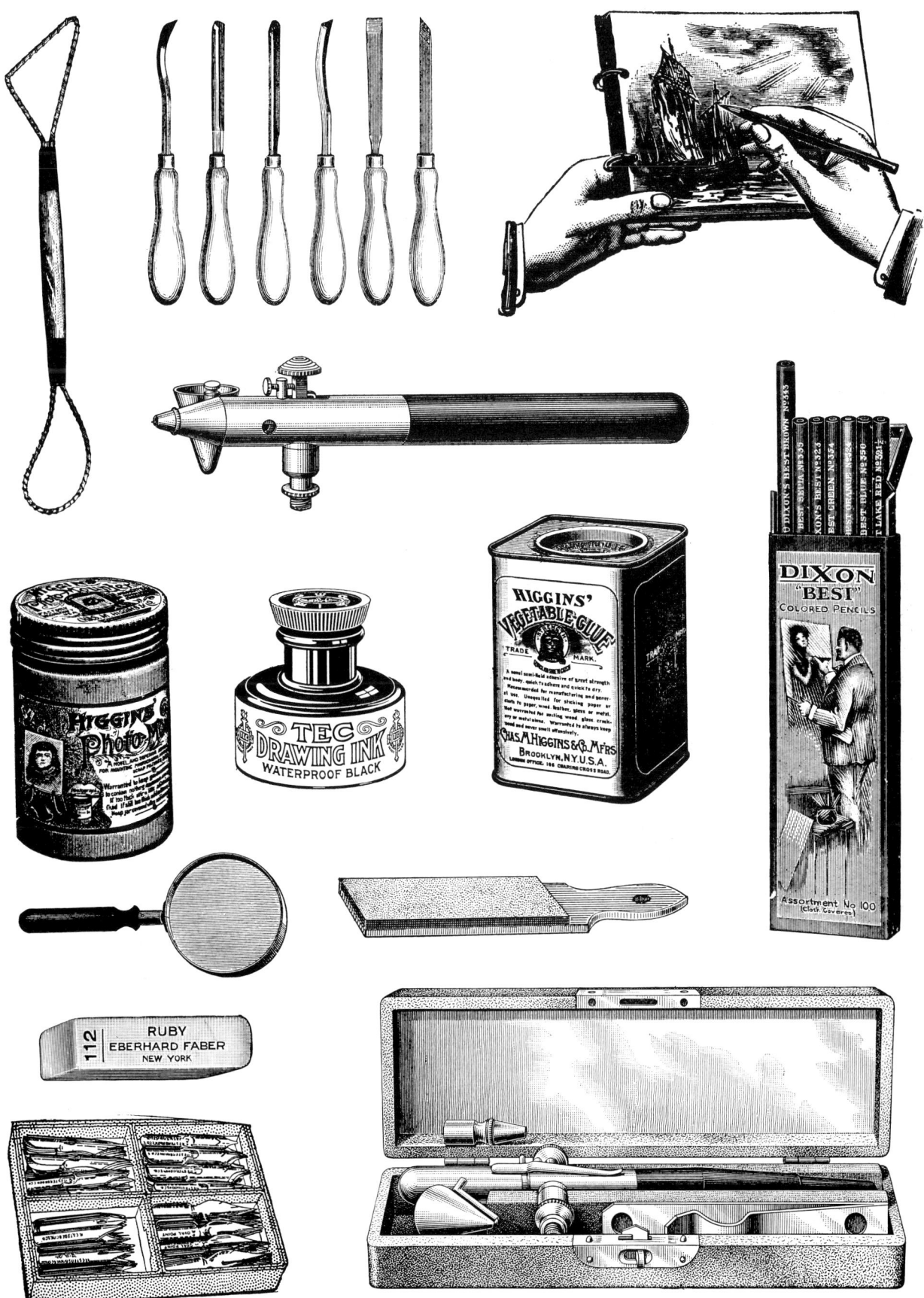

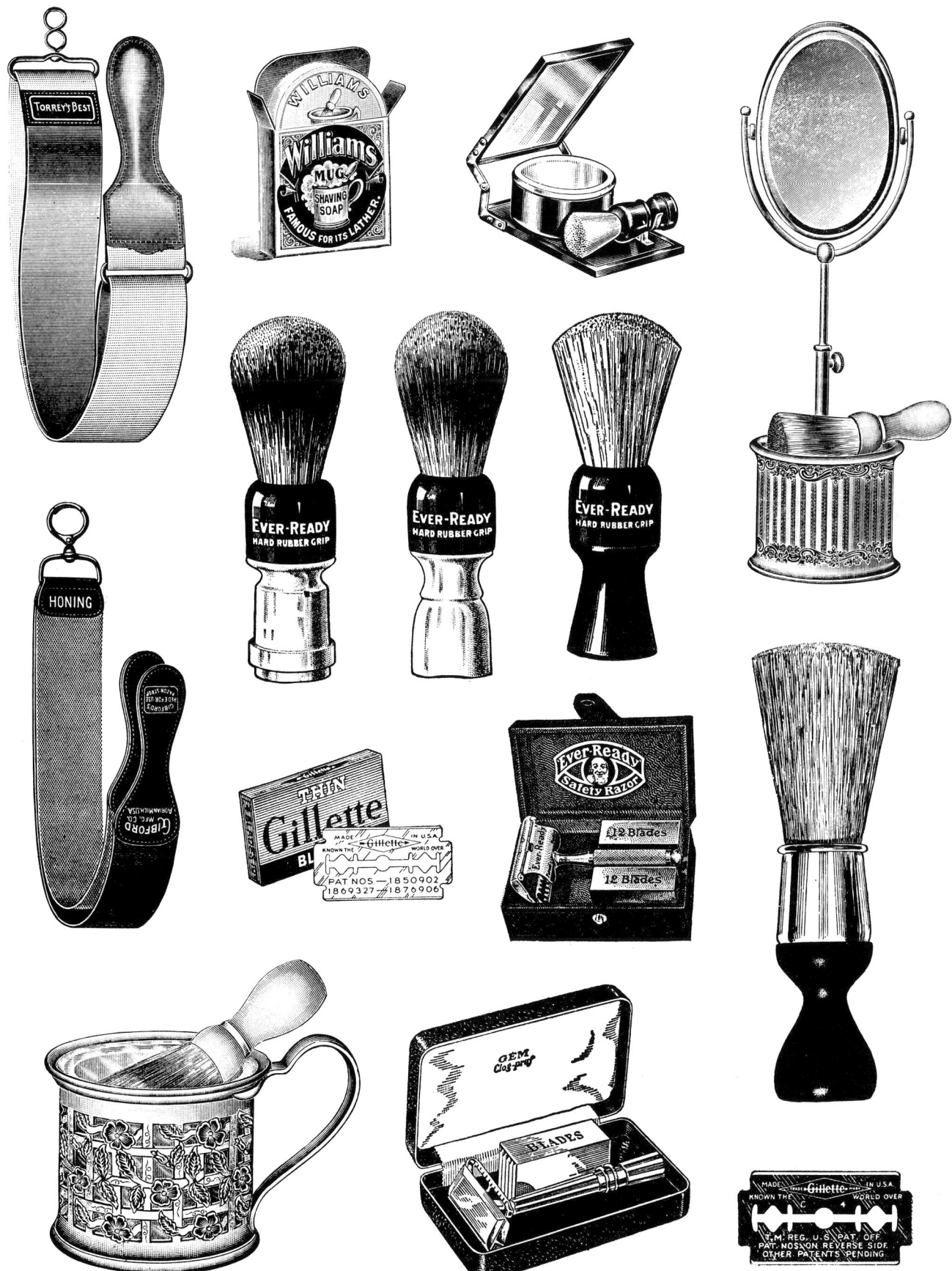

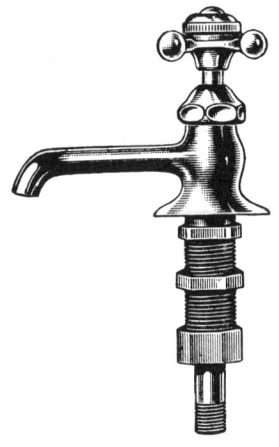
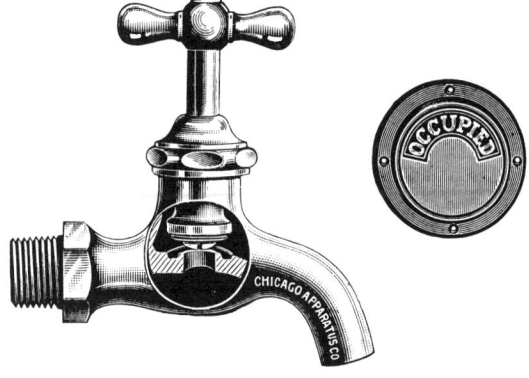

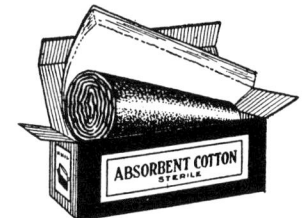

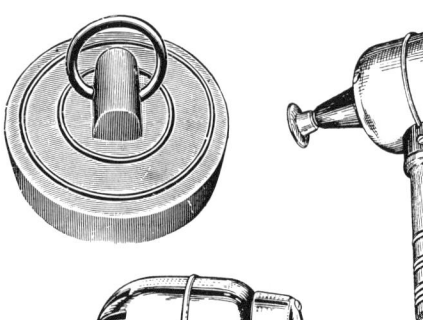

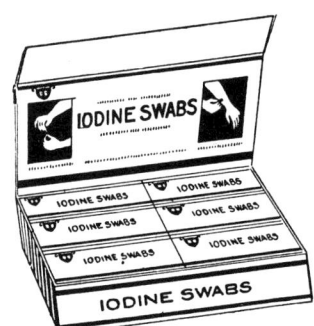

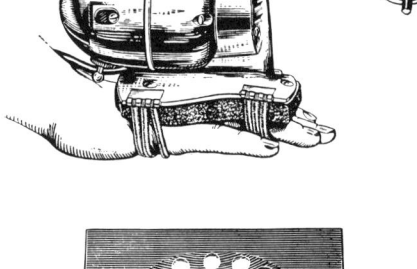

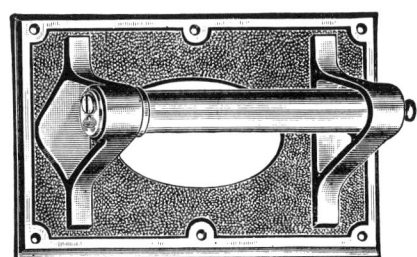

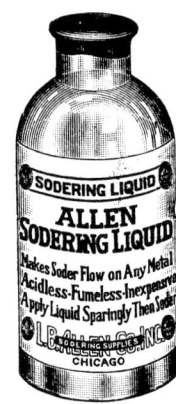

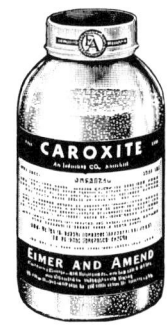

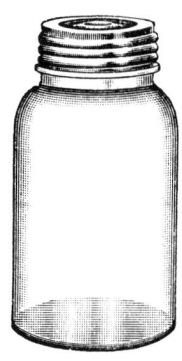

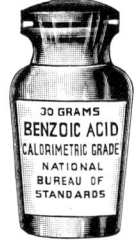

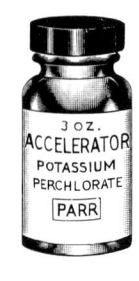

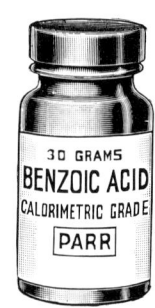

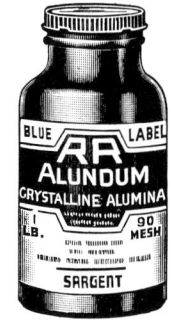
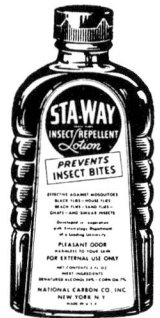

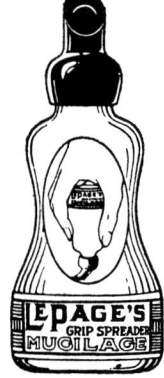
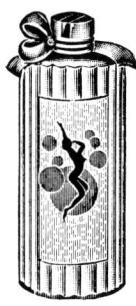

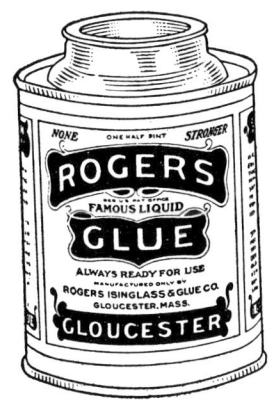

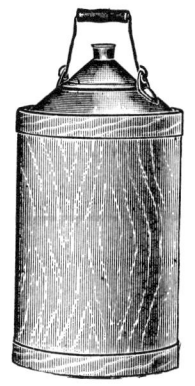

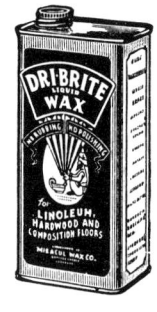

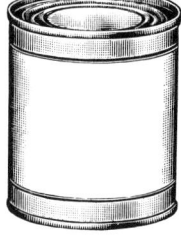

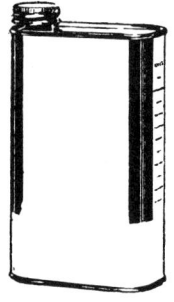
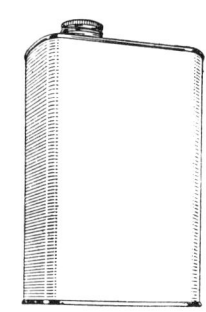

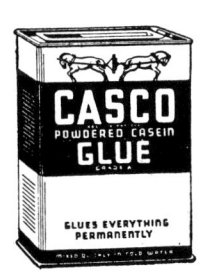

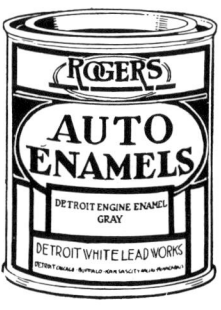

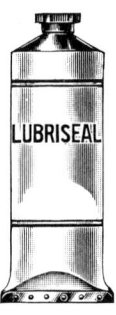

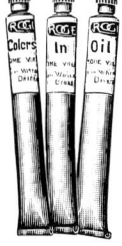

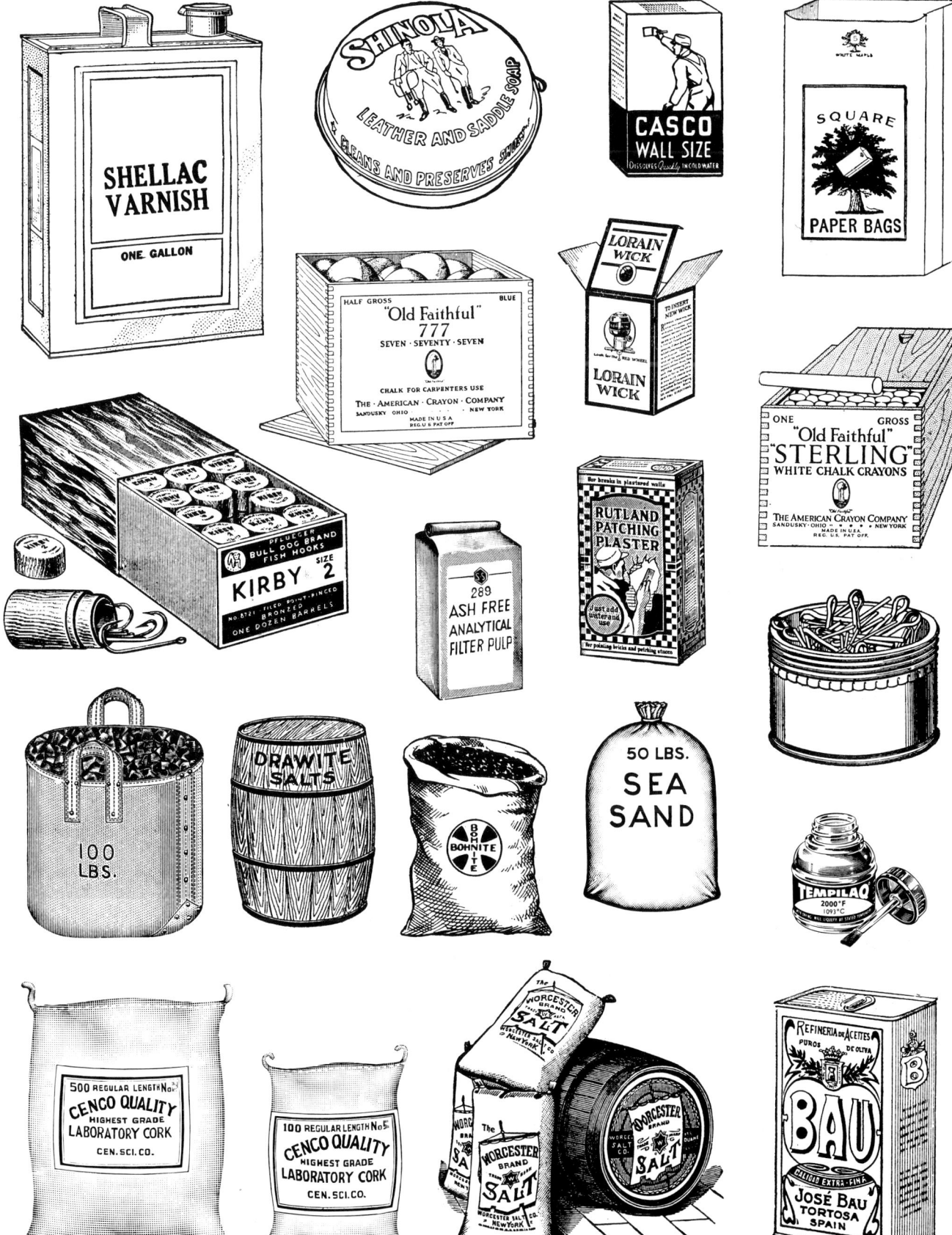

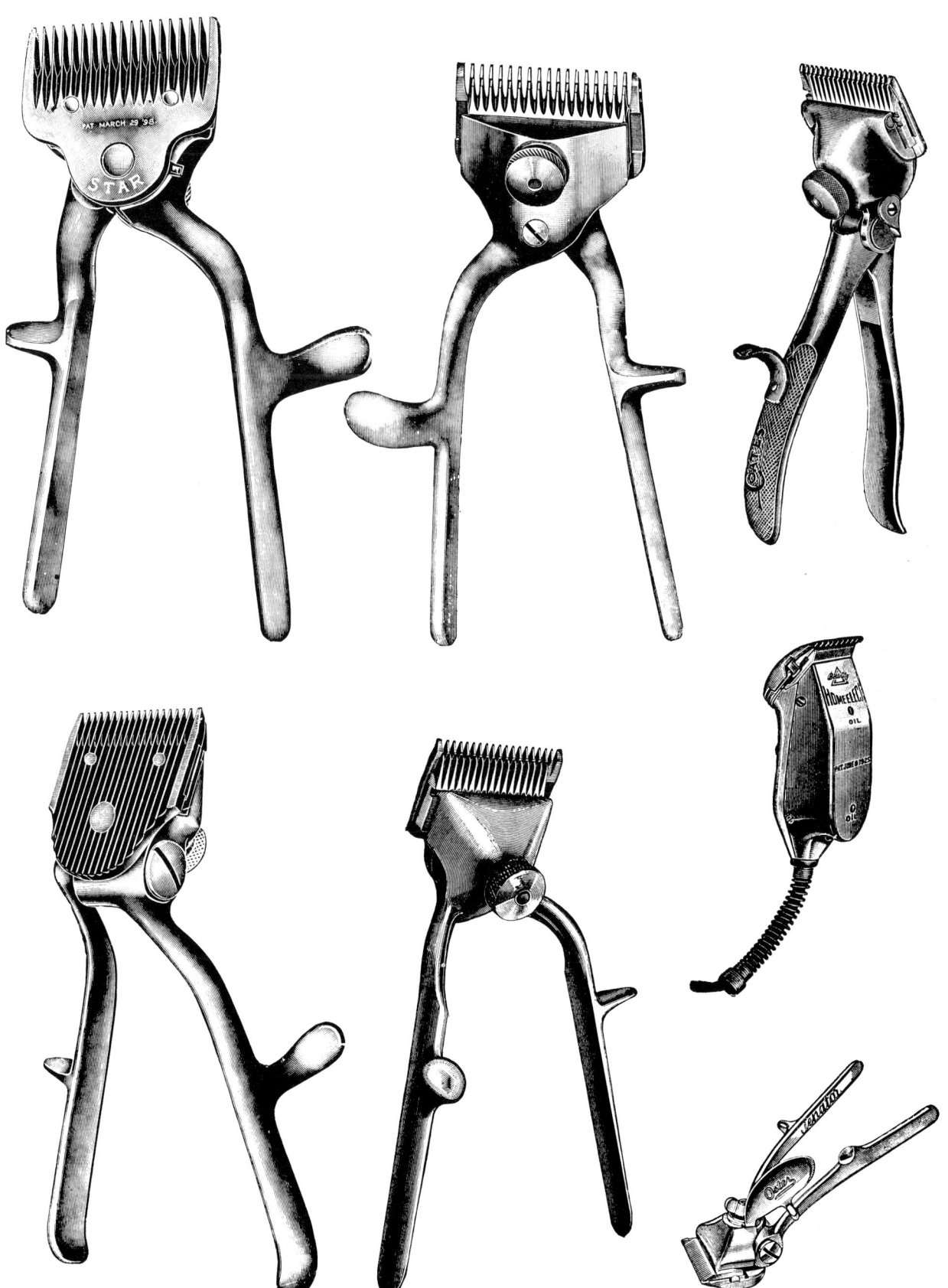

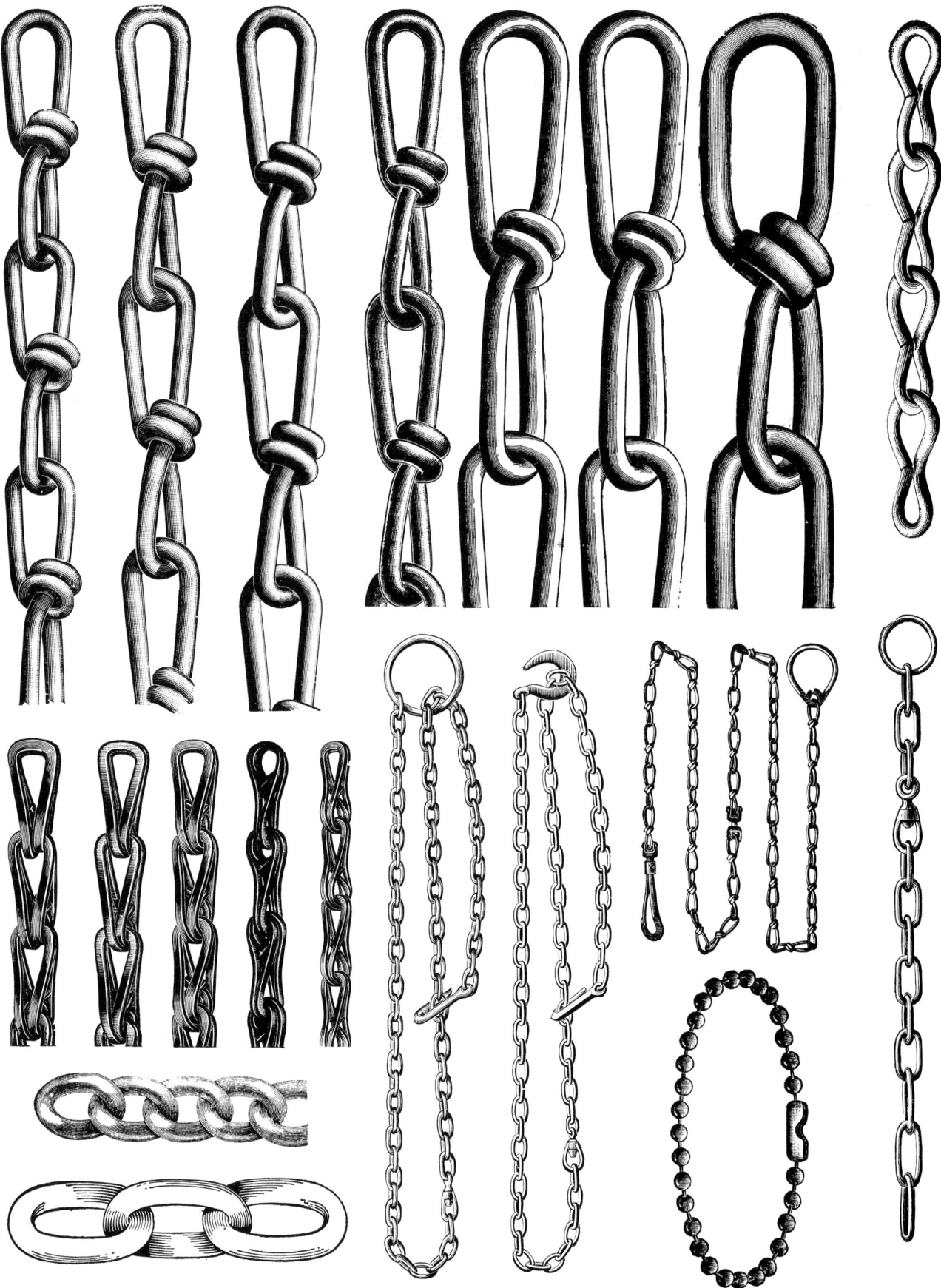

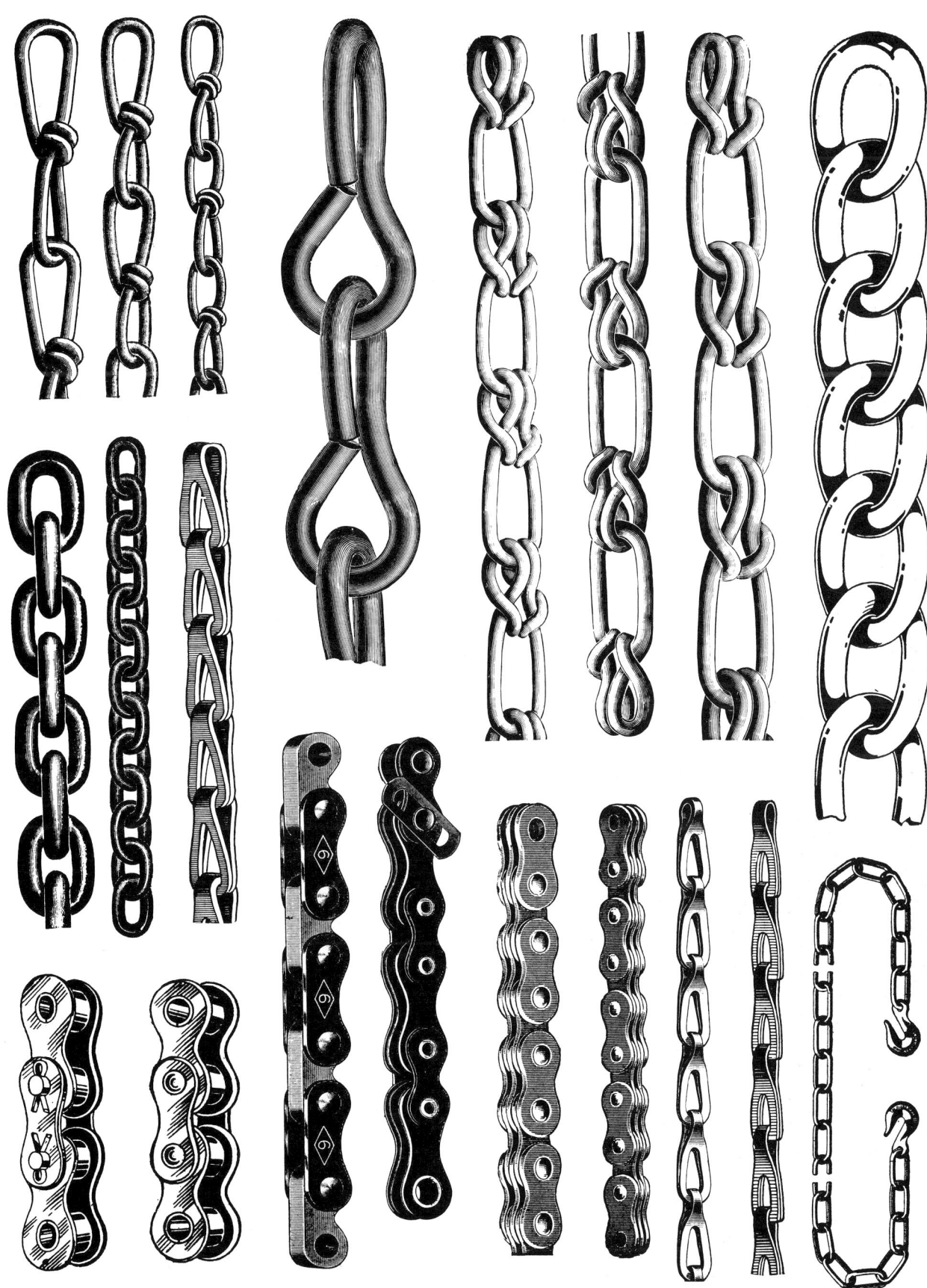

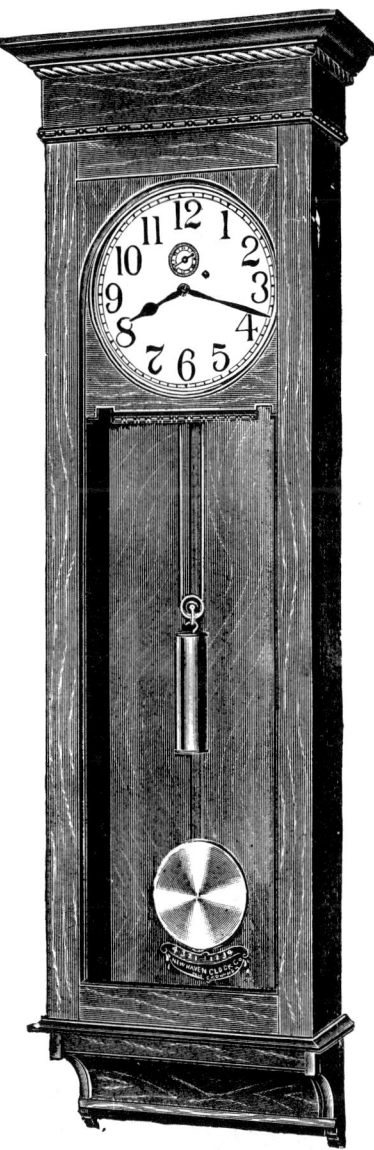

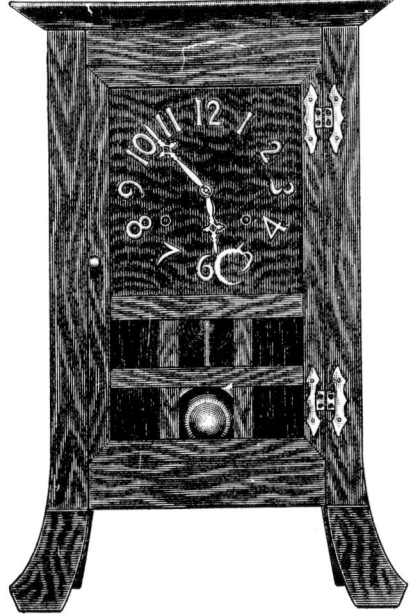

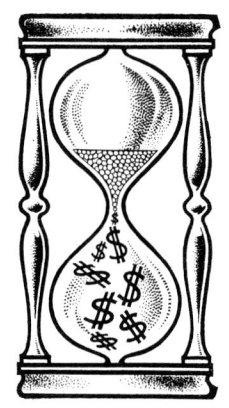

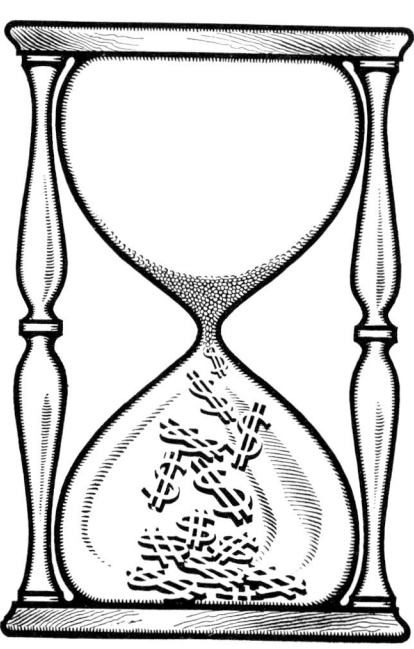

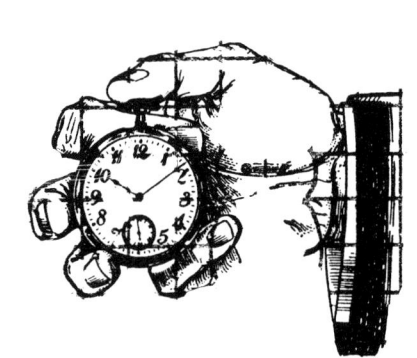

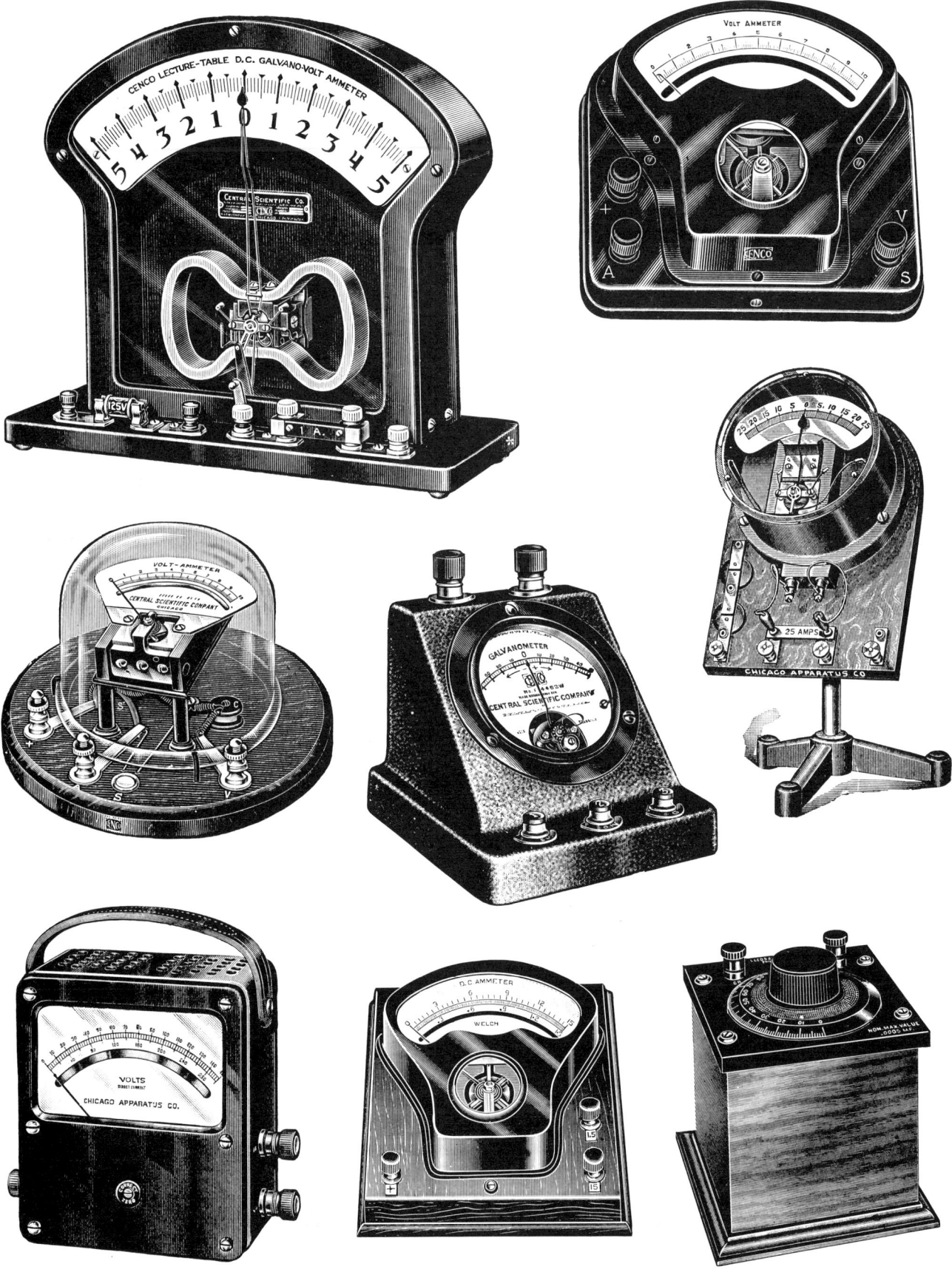

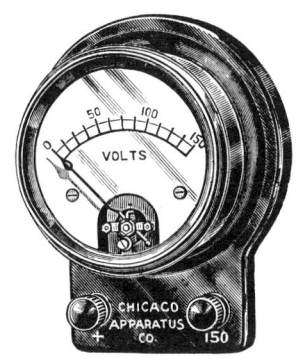

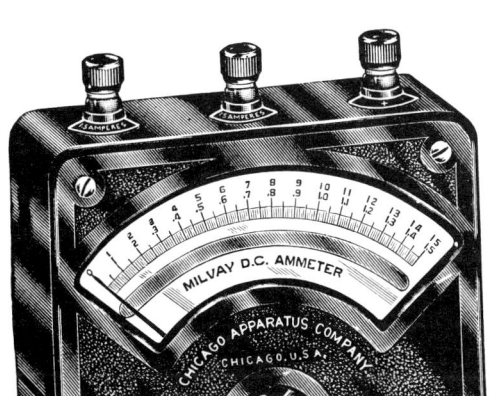

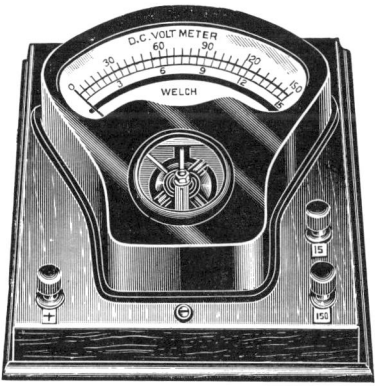

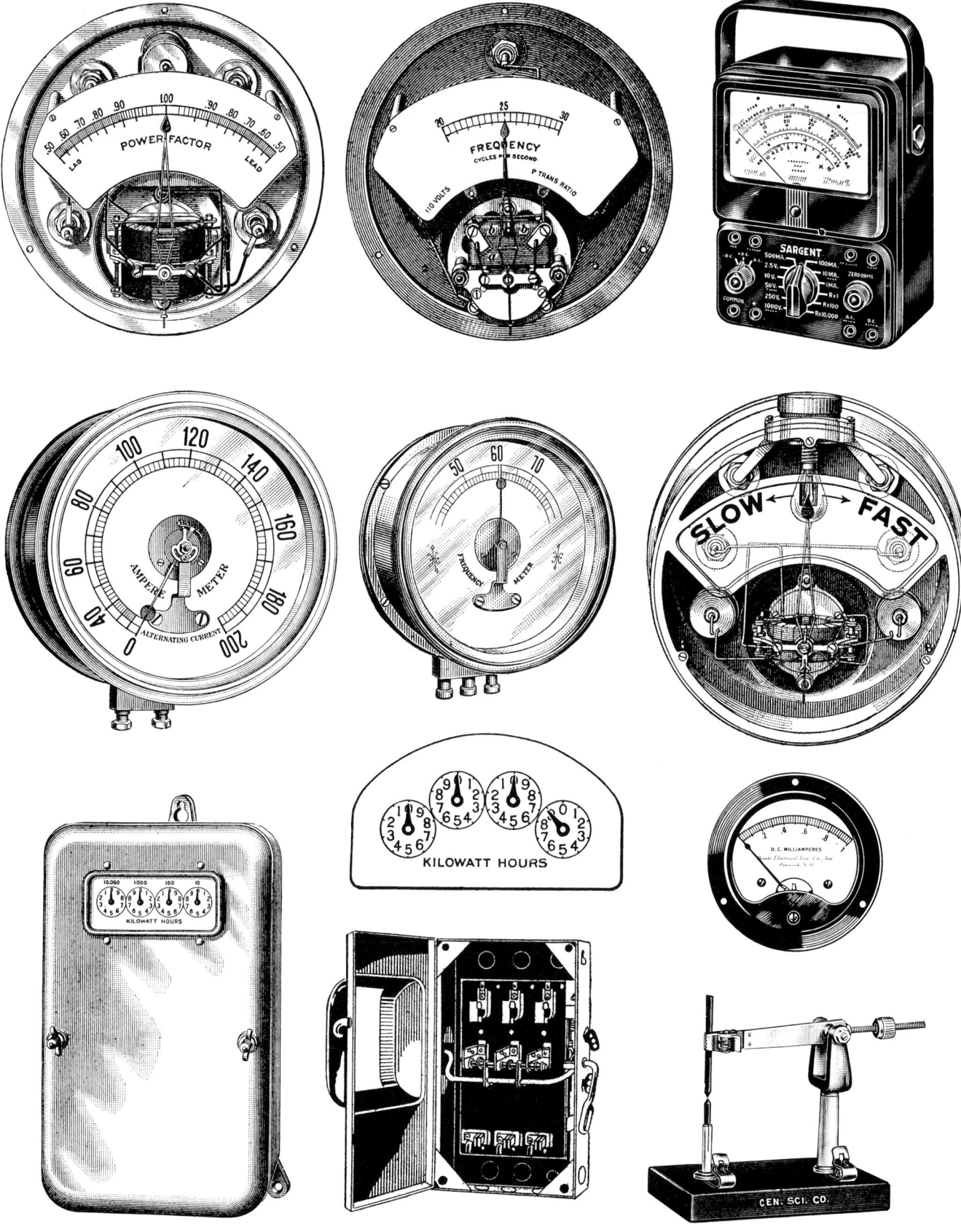

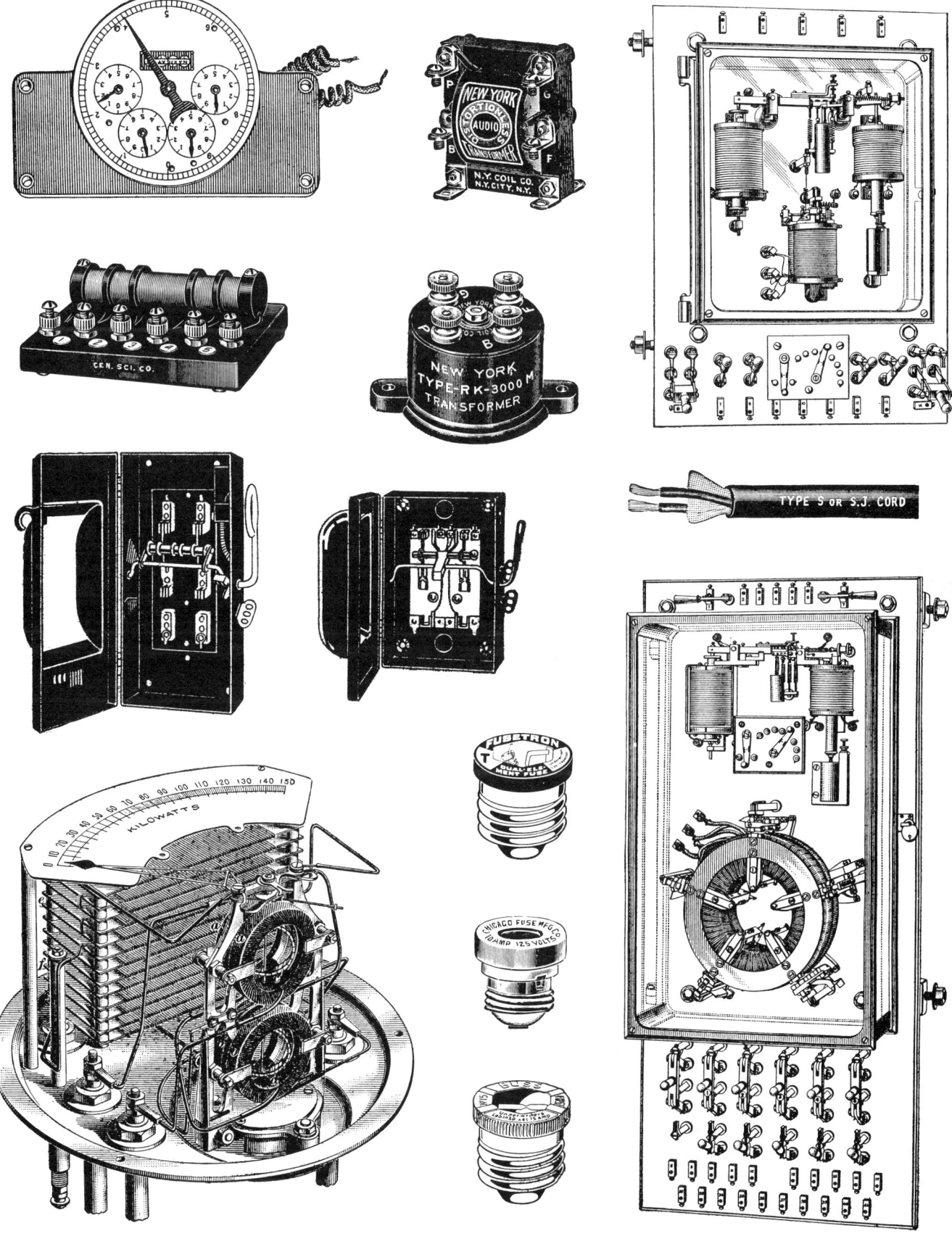

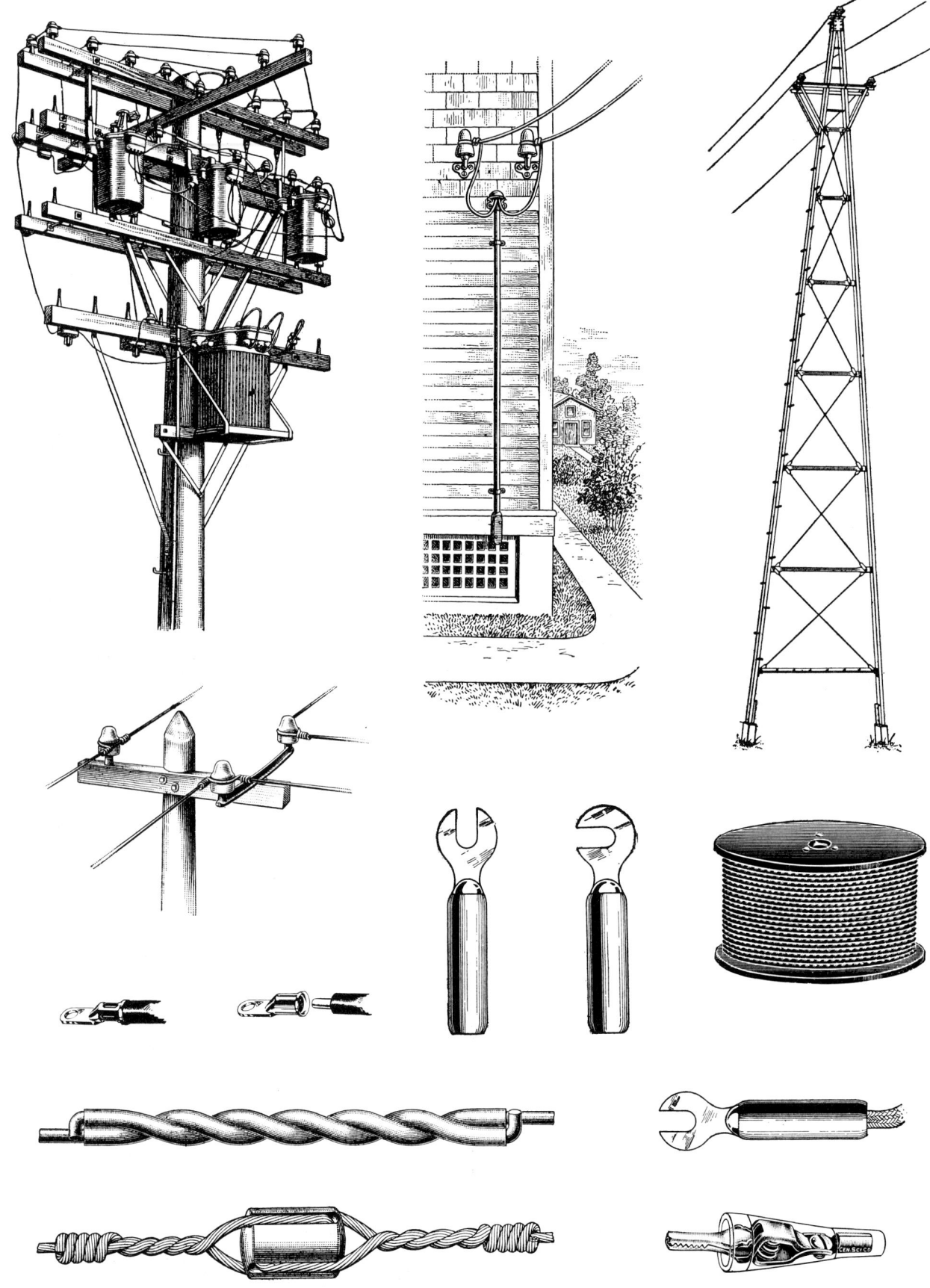

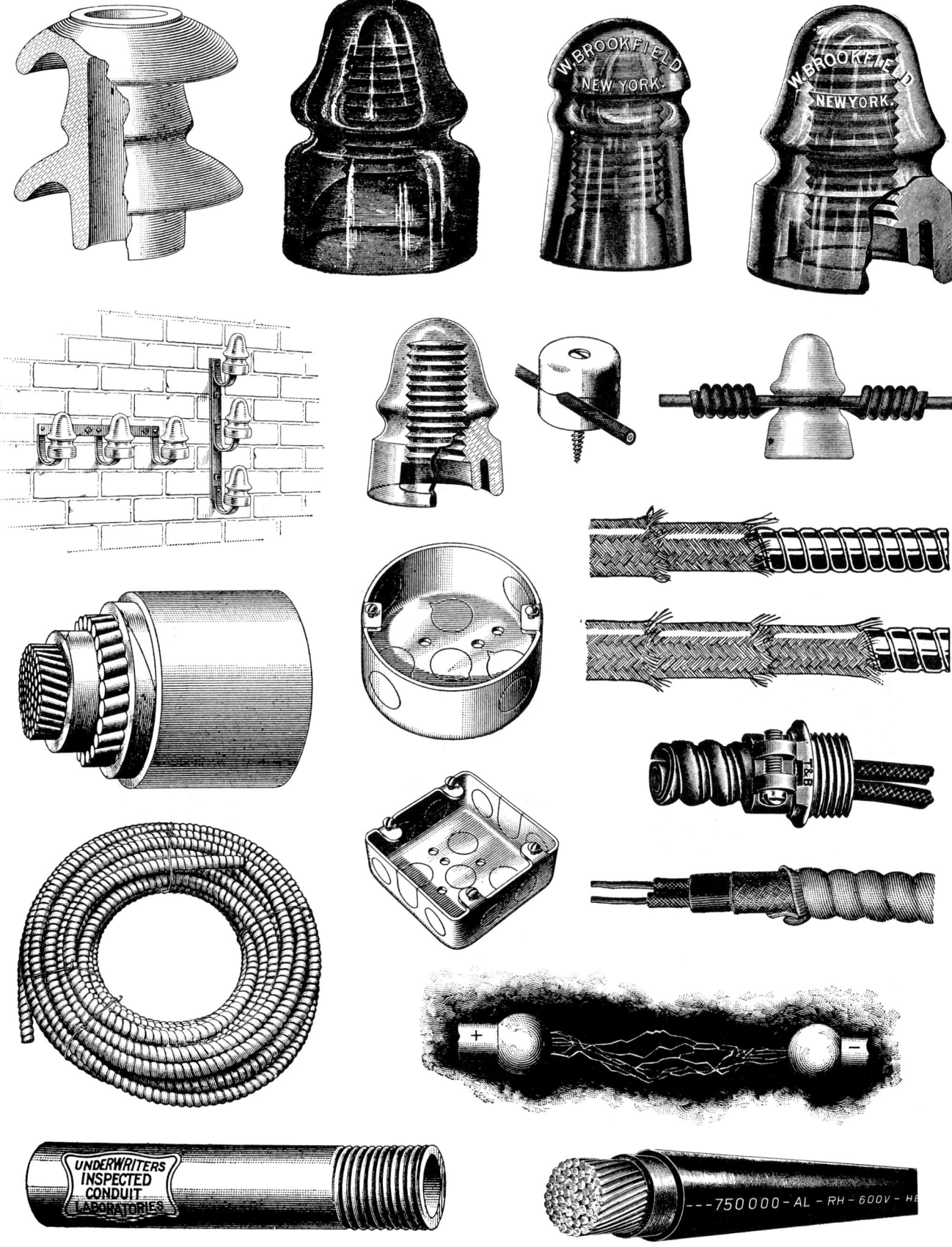

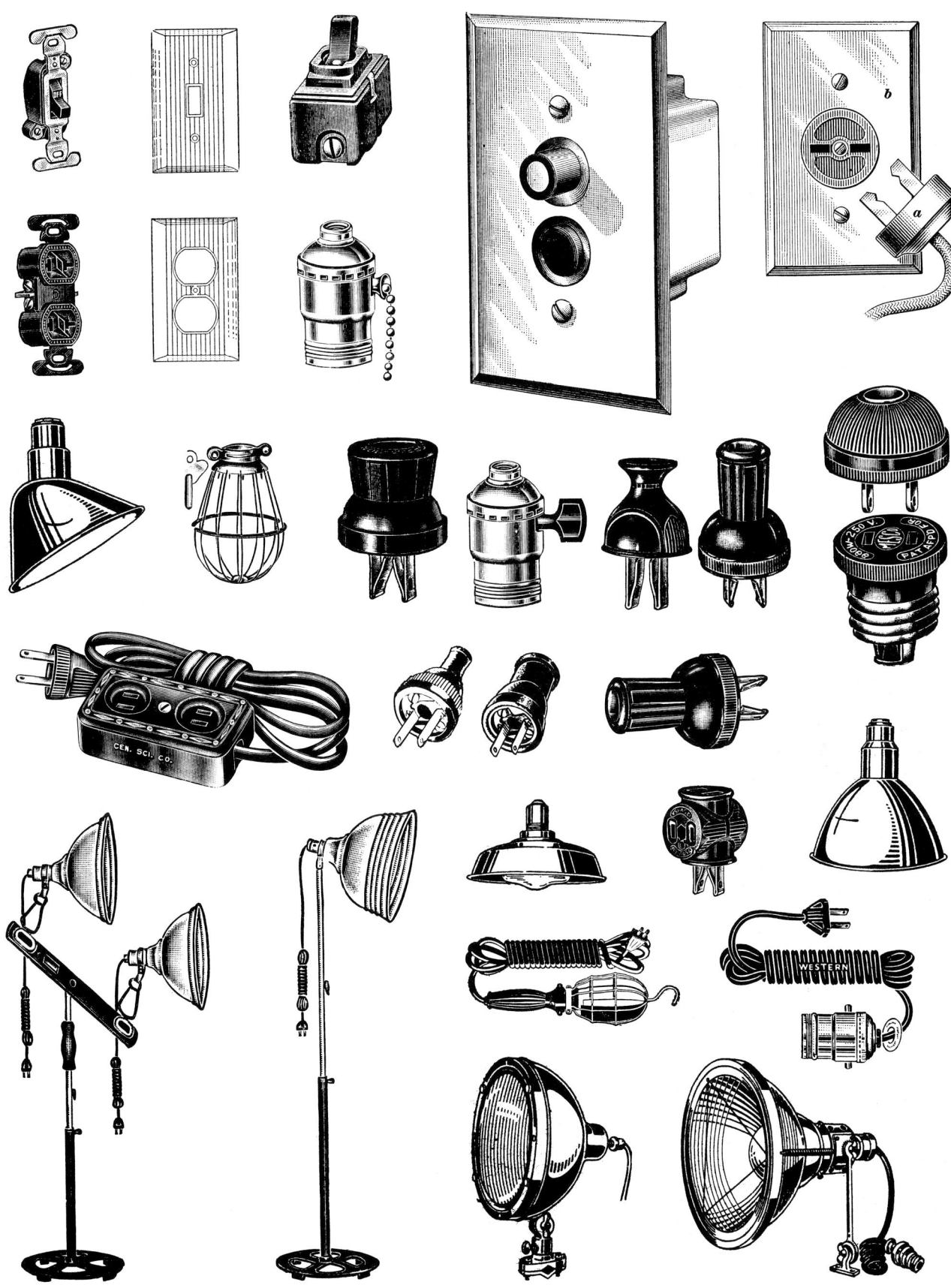

EVEREADY
EVEREADY
BOND
No 6
DRY CELL
BUILT FOR
HEAVY DUTY
IGNITION-RADIO
SERVICE
BOND ELECTRIC CORPORATION
NEW HAVEN, CONN.
MADE IN U.S.A.
EVEREADY
BURGESS
4FH
BURGESS
S461
No 935
EVEREADY
UNIT CELL
FOR FLASHLIGHTS
NATIONAL CARBON CO.
NEW YORK, N.Y.
MADE IN U.S.A.
NO.7
Willard
BOND
MADE IN U.S.A.
SUPER SERVICE SAFETY SEAL
BOND
NO. 102 SIZE "D"
SUPER-SERVICE
MONO-CELL
FLASHLIGHT BATTERY
BOND
No 123
LANTERN
BATTERY
BOND ELECTRIC CORPORATION
NEW HAVEN CONN.
CHICAGO · SAN FRANCISCO
BURGESS
NO.6
MALLORY
RM-42 R
SARGENT
MALLORY
TR236R
SARGENT
MALLORY
FOR
RADIO AND
TRANSISTOR
APPLICATIONS
TR-146

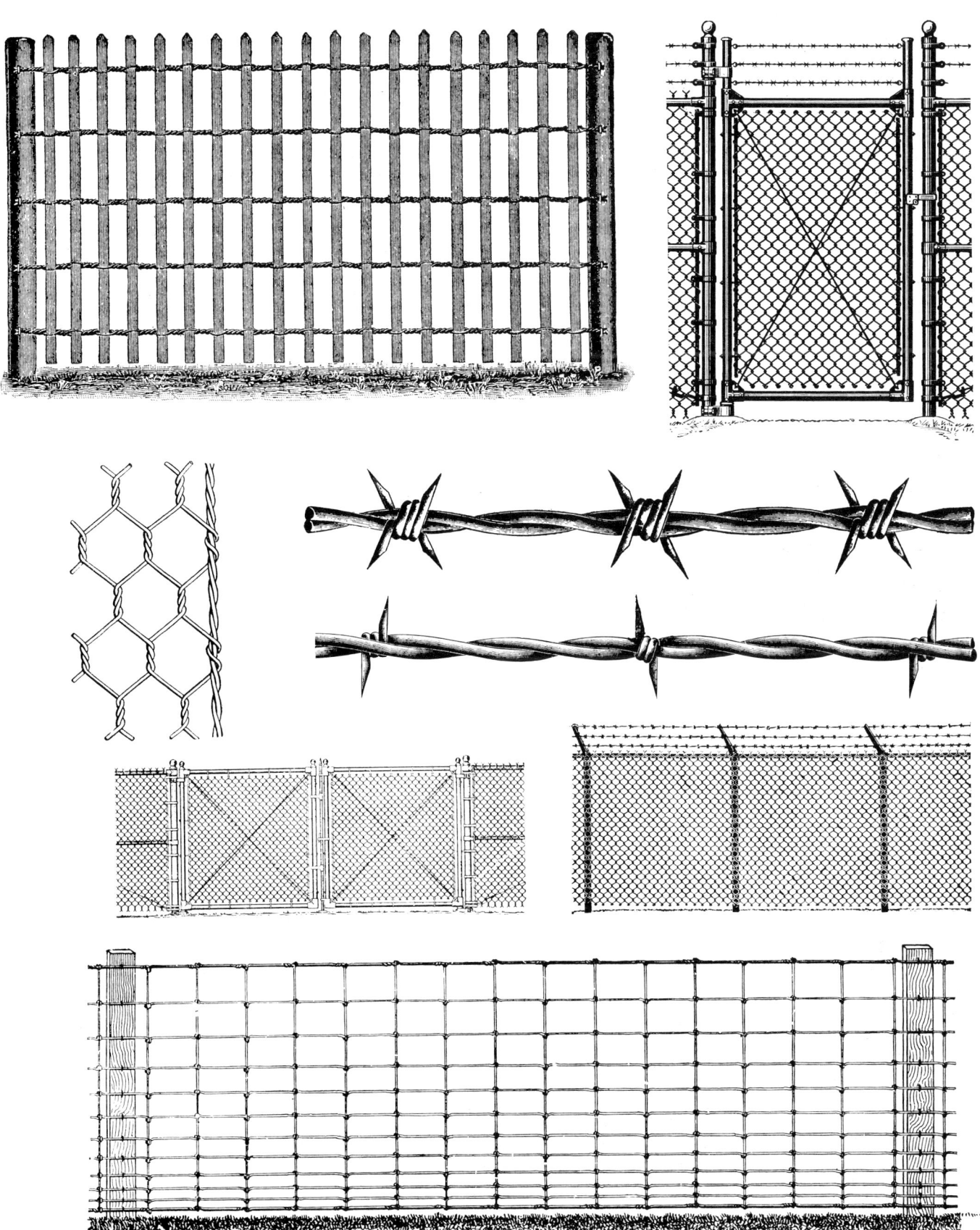

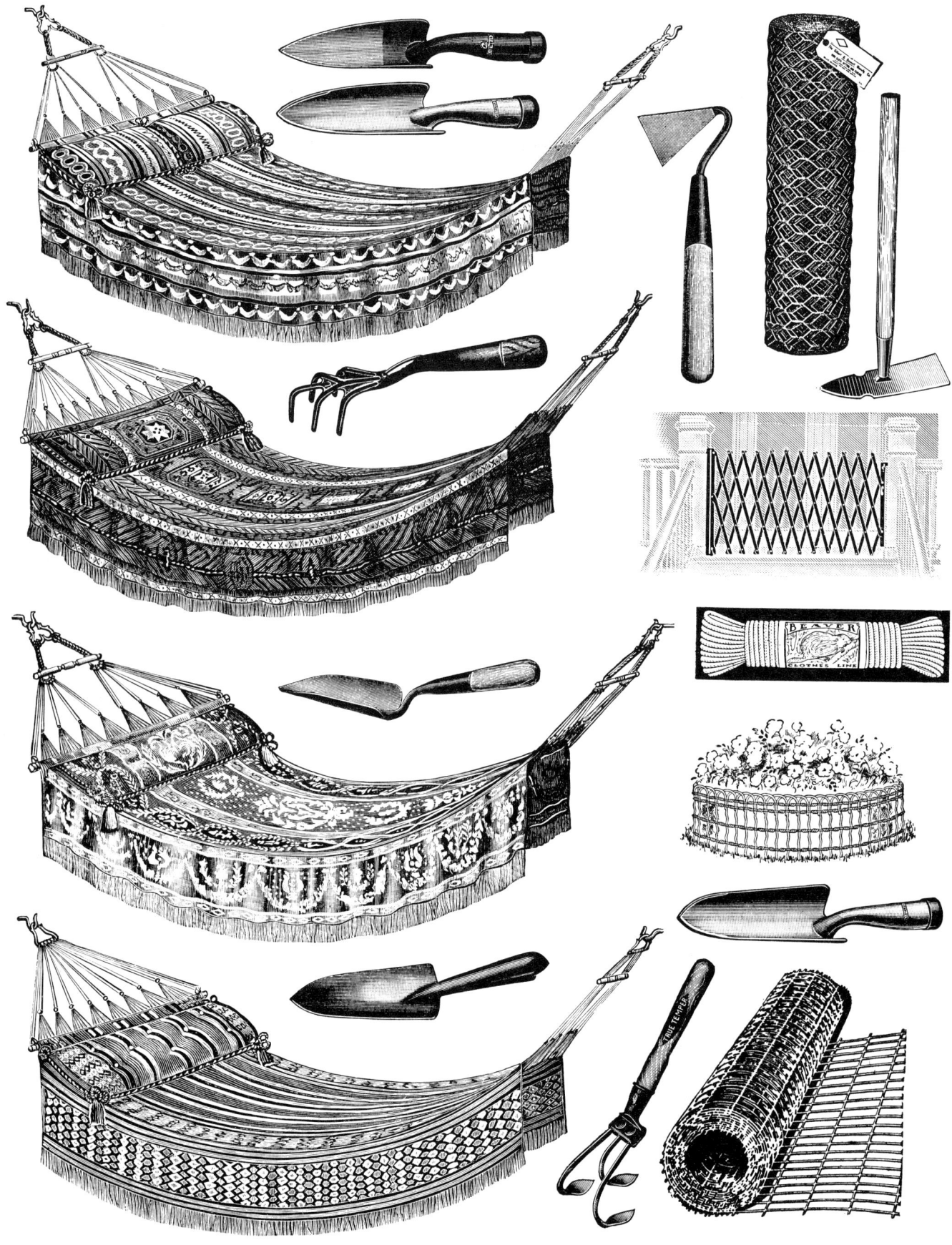

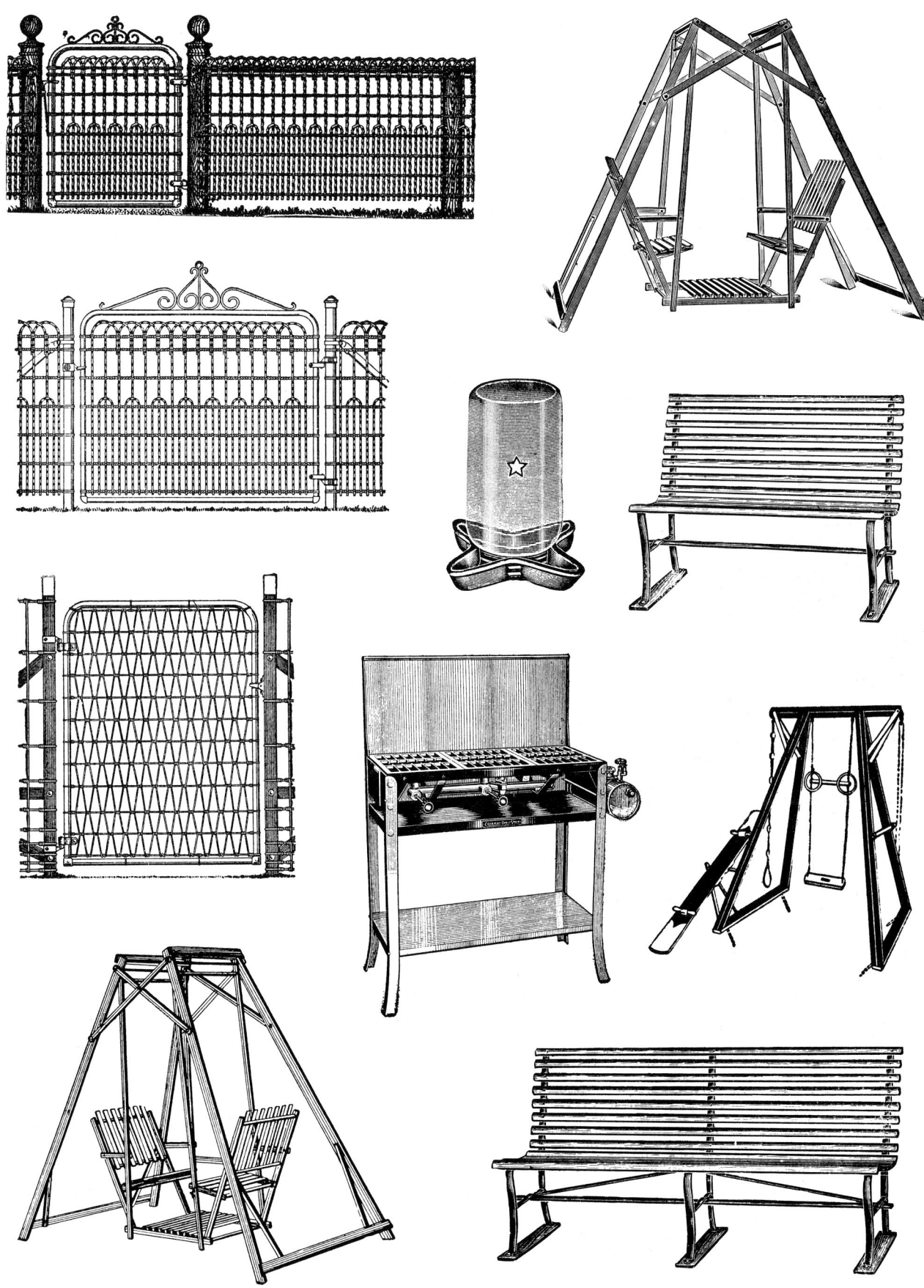

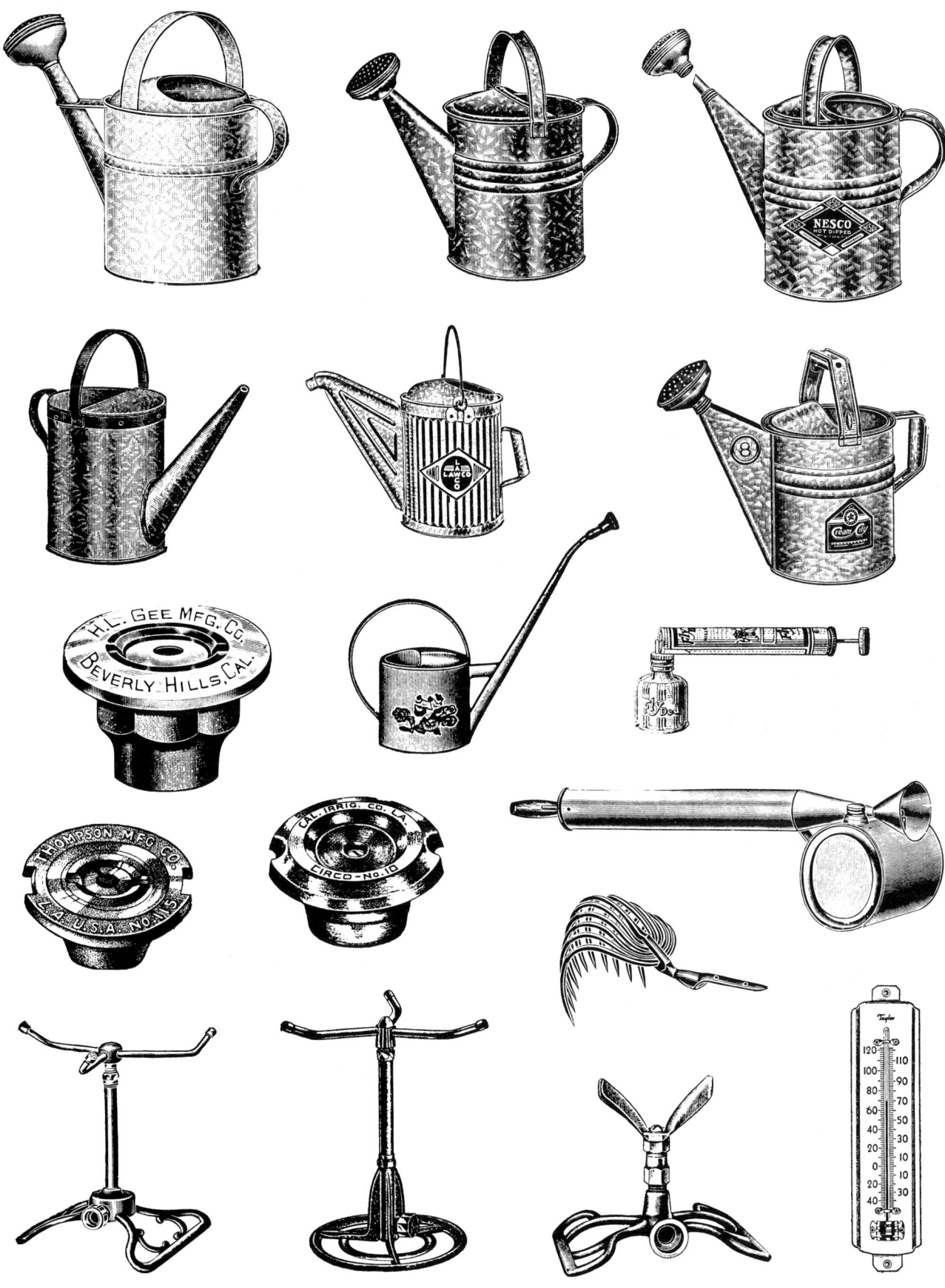

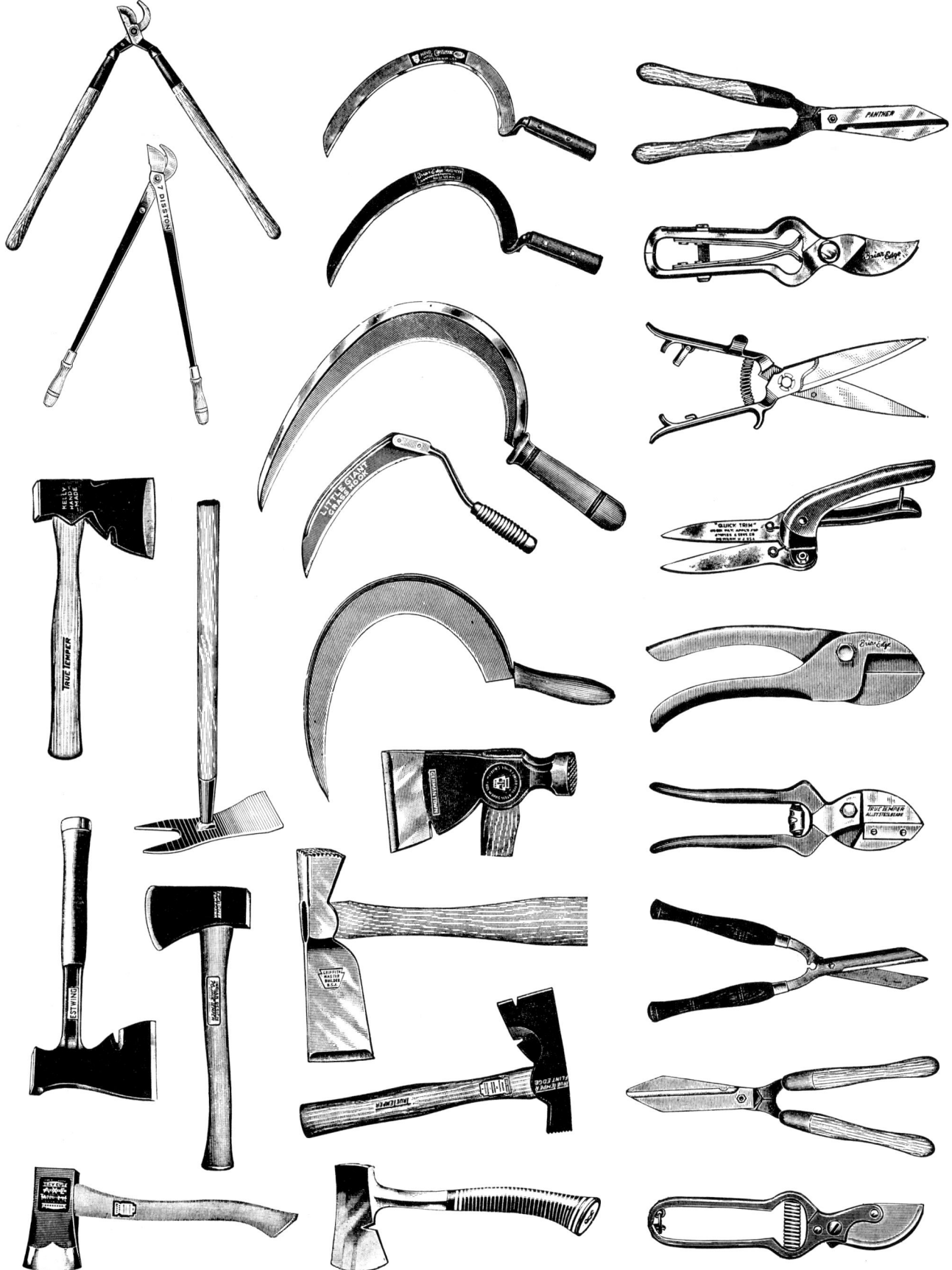

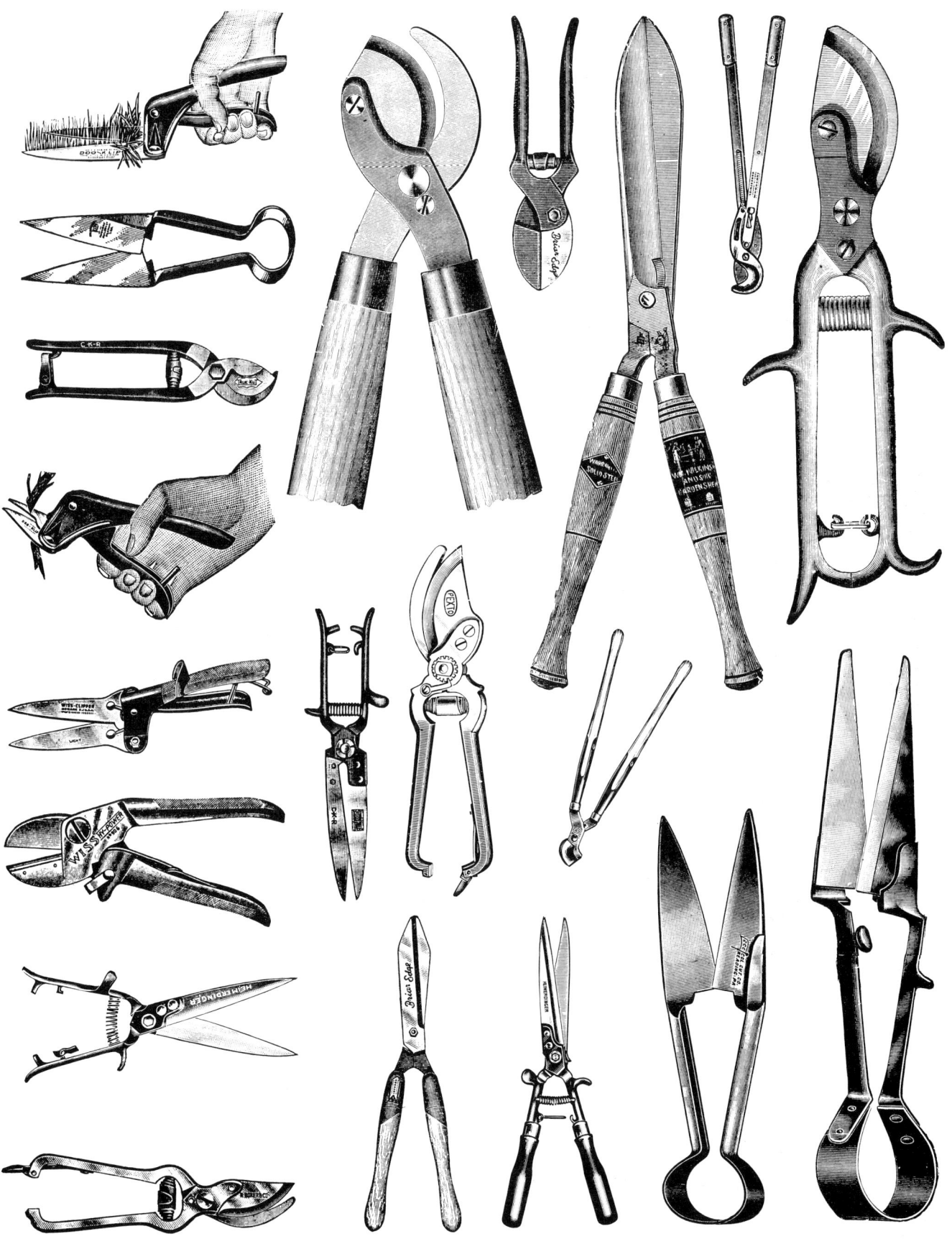

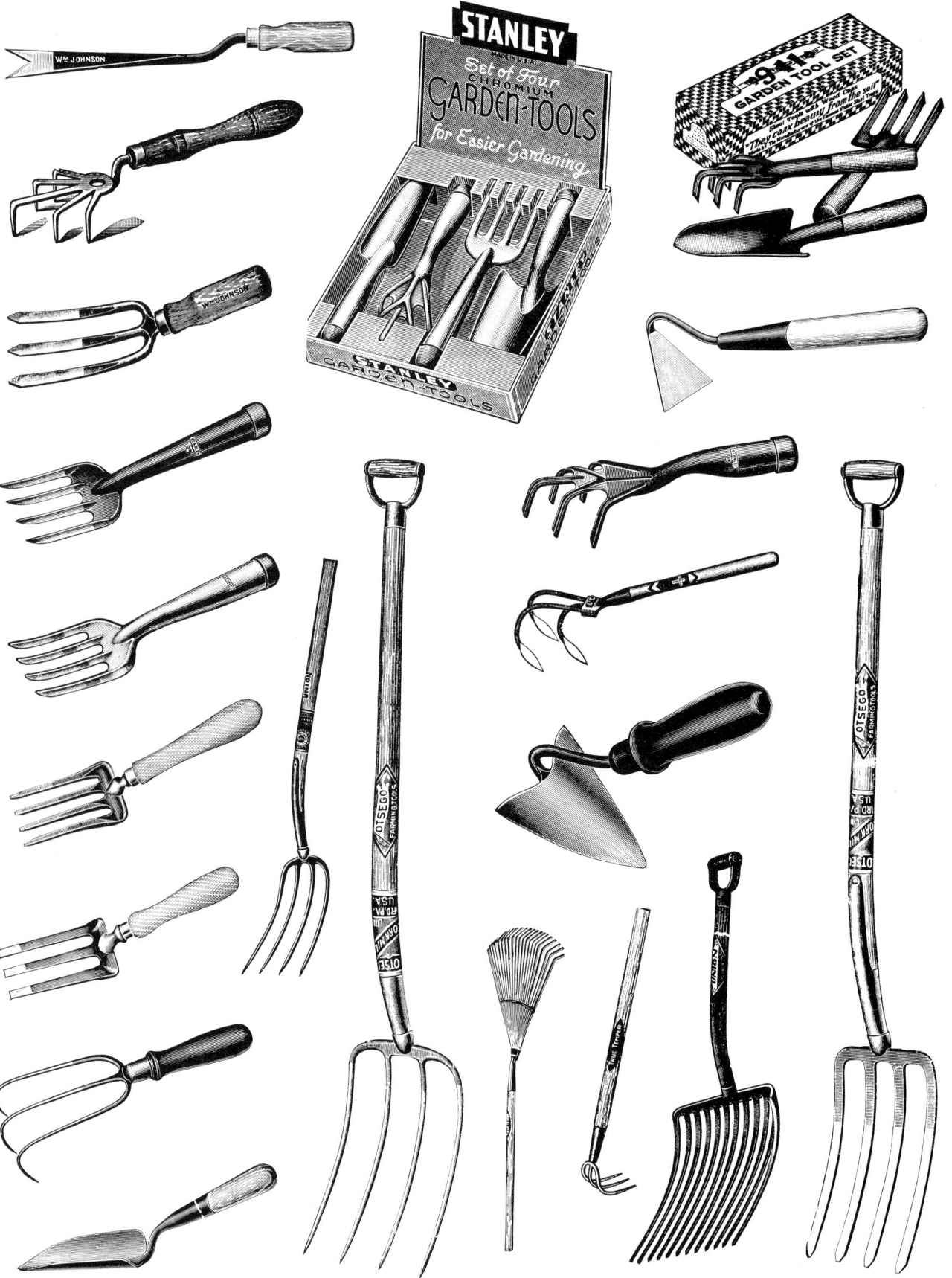

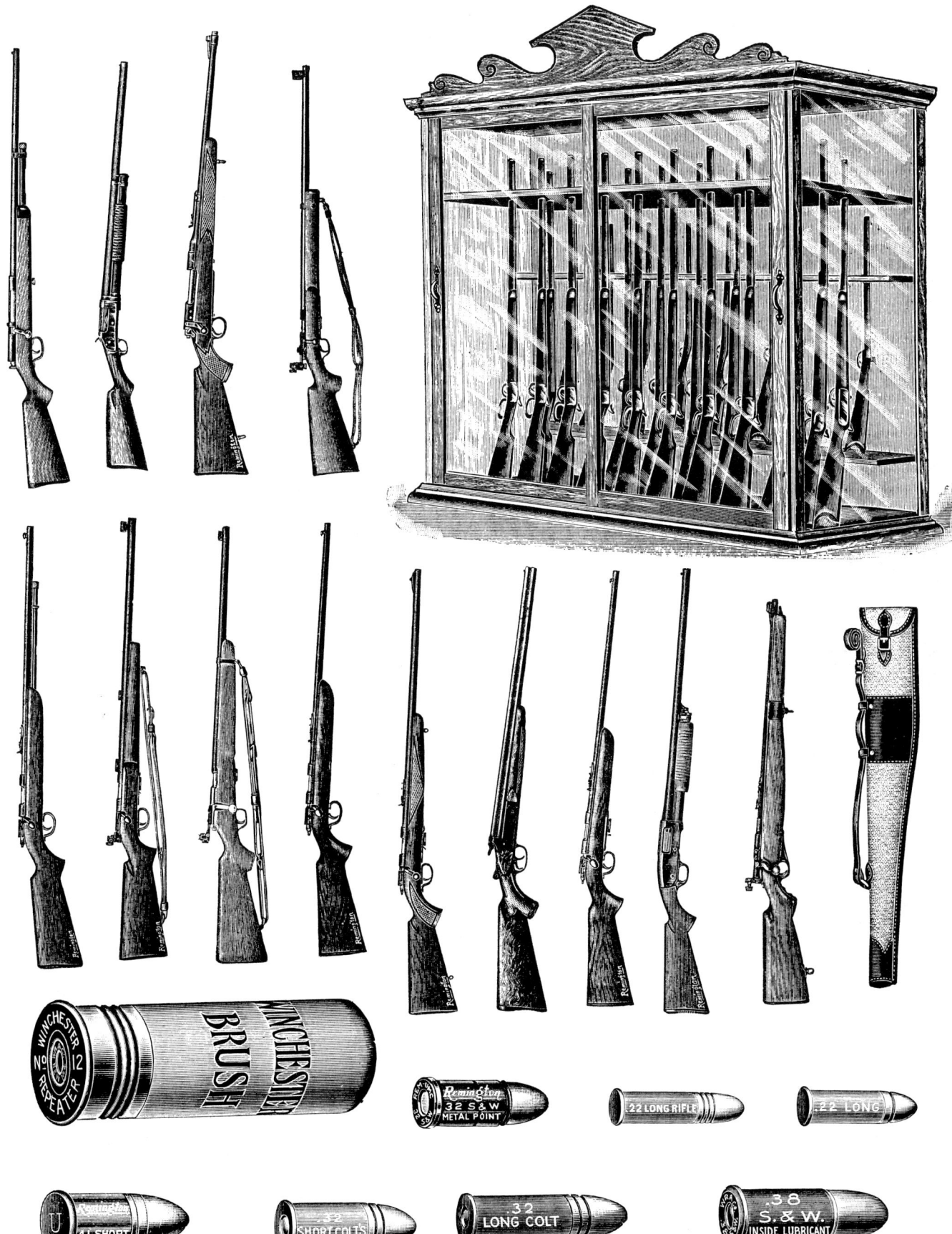

Index